7 7 7!

Seven Curses - Seven Sprinklings - Seven Blessings

7 Curses brought woe.

7 Sprinklings bring wholeness.

7 Blessings release abundance!

*Invoking the Blood Jesus Shed in Seven Places
To Break Seven Curses and Release Seven Blessings.*

Dr. Douglas E. Carr

Copyright © 2024 Douglas E. Carr

All rights reserved, though permission is granted to those using it in ministry to use anything within.

ISBN: 978-1-7366952-8-9

Bible Translations Used

Except where noted, the Scripture comes from the:

📖 New King James Version®. Copyright © 1982 by Thomas Nelson. Used by permission. All rights reserved.

Other Bible Translations used include:

📖 Amplified Bible (AMP) Copyright © 2015 by The Lockman Foundation, La Habra, CA 90631. All rights reserved.
📖 Amplified Bible, Classic Edition (AMPC) Copyright © 1954, 1958, 1962, 1964, 1965, 1987 by The Lockman Foundation
📖 American Standard Version (ASV) Public Domain
📖 DARBY Public Domain
📖 King James Version (KJV) by Public Domain
📖 New American Standard Bible (NASB) Copyright © 1960, 1962, 1963, 1968, 1971, 1972, 1973, 1975, 1977, 1995 by The Lockman Foundation
📖 The Message (MSG) Copyright © 1993, 2002, 2018 by Eugene H. Peterson.
📖 New International Version (NIV) Holy Bible, New International Version®, NIV® Copyright ©1973, 1978, 1984, 2011 by Biblica, Inc.® Used by permission. All rights reserved worldwide.

ENDORSEMENTS

It has been a pleasure to know Dr. Doug Carr. Through my mother, I was first able to meet Pastor Carr many years ago. Since then, he has been dedicated to pouring into my family, church, and non-profit ministry. As a public speaker who has visited many churches, I can attest of the presence of The Holy Spirit when you enter through the doors of his church. His wisdom exudes through each book he writes. His latest, 7 7 7 has been no different. As I turned each page, I was challenged in my faith and discovered new truths through his descriptive guidance. It has been my utmost privilege to sit under his leadership and wisdom. I am so thankful he is a part of our community. He is a pillar of strength and knowledge that many turn to, or refer others to, in times of trouble. His teacher's heart has a passion for others' spiritual growth, evidenced through each encounter and book he writes.

It is with great enthusiasm I continue in his circle of growth, and I am able to recommend 7 7 7.

Tiffany Wagler
Co- Founder and Executive Director
Rooted of St. Joseph County, Inc.

It is my privilege to meet with Dr. Douglas Carr and some other Kingdom pastors each month to pray for our community and the Kingdom work in our churches. This wonderful experience has given me insight into this man's heart for God and people. As pastors, we are well aware of the brokenness of people whom we have the opportunity to minister. We have seen how Jesus has made lives new that were broken. It was Jesus who said, "behold I make all things new." Through the power and the work of the Holy Spirit, the "woes" in this life are changed to "wows" for the glory of God. This is no small thing, my friend.

Over the years, Doug has helped countless people come to know the freedom that only comes through Jesus. He has helped them learn to walk and live in their new freedom by understanding that once set free from Satan's hold they are to live in the power of the Holy Spirit.

Doug's latest book, 7 7 7 will be a blessing to all who read and apply the truth within its pages. Chapter eleven, "Praying It All the Way Through" is powerful, as is Chapter seven where Doug compares human hands being used for blessings or curses. 7 7 7 is a book showing the way from a broken and captive life to a life which has been set free, all for the glory of God. When the title of this book is lived out, people will be in awe of God and truly be blessed!

Rev. Bob L Renner
Sturgis, Michigan

DEDICATION

I dedicate this book to Pamela Jo Musselman-Carr who is my best friend, wife, and partner in life and ministry. Only the Holy Spirit has taught me more about living a life of love, grace, continuing victory, and sacrificial living than she. Pam is my favorite hero!

Early in our marriage, Pam and I began reading the Bible out loud to each other every morning. Each year we read through the Old Testament once, and the New Testament twice. Even though I had previously read through the Bible many times, it came alive in new ways because of her ability to enter the storylines as we read. Some of her observations are practical and simple, like when we were reading about Old Testament sacrifices. I never got much out of them until one morning when she said, "It must be God likes the smell of a good barbeque." She also noted the importance of the number seven as used in sprinkling the blood of sacrificial offerings.

Pam shares other observations that rock my boat to the point I must hang on tighter to Jesus. Only then do I understand the deeper levels of what God is still speaking. As a prophet and seer, Pam often gets to the heart of what God is saying and shares things I have missed through over five decades of study.

I also dedicate this book to people who simply are done with low living and ready to advance the Kingdom of God! May God increase His army who will apply the work of Calvary to break every curse and step into every blessing God wants His children to enjoy through the completed work of Jesus' death, burial, resurrection, and ascension into heaven.

May we become increasingly godlike and make Jesus famous!

Acknowledgements

The Lord is so good to me. He has surrounded me with people whom He uses to teach me and help me press further into His Kingdom. Our congregation at His House Foursquare Church, willingly share me with others by giving me time to write, minister deliverance, and lead seminars and equipping programs.

The Reach the Forgotten chaplains and inmates at the Branch County Jail provide me opportunity to see if these truths apply to everyone who is open to Holy Spirit ministry, whether walking in freedom or incarcerated in jail.

Michiana Apostolic Strike force (southwest Michigan and Northeast Indiana) is a team of apostles, prophets, evangelists, pastors, and Teachers. We are on assignment together and carry an atmosphere of faith and intercession that lift us higher each month.

Suzanne LeBlanc has been a wonderful help in countless ways. She proofreads my books, edits them, rescues me from countless computer issues that seem to plague me. Her countless hours in formatting my books and providing helpful thoughts and hints are priceless!

Above all else, God Almighty is the source of everything good I do and write. He assigned a scribe angel to me in 2019. I have never seen the angel manifest, but my writing takes on a whole new depth and meaning when he is engaged. John Maxwell said, "If you see a turtle sitting on a fencepost, you know it did not get there by himself." I readily give God and the people He put in my life the credit for the books I write.

Contents

	Foreword by Cindy Williams Moore	11
	Preface	15
	Introduction	17
1	An Interesting Key	29
2	Sprinkle Seven Times	39
3	Tale of Two Gardens	49
4	Healing Through His Stripes	65
5	Taking Back Freedom Through His Bruises	75
6	Taking Hold of Prosperity Through His Thorns	87
	Addendum on Prosperity	101
7	Taking Back Success Through His Hands	105
8	Taking Back Dominion Through His Feet	115
9	Taking Back Wholeness Through His Heart	127
	May Hearts Dare to Beat Again	138
10	Praying it All the Way Through	141
11	The Devil's Attempt to Obscure the Power of the Blood	147
12	Tree of Life vs Tree of Knowledge	159
	About the Author	180
	Resources	181

Foreword by Cindy Williams Moore
7 7 7! – 7 CURSES, 7 SPRINKLINGS, 7 BLESSINGS

Walk with me for a few minutes while I share the value of the book you hold in your hands, how it impacted me, and will affect you and position you to run your race strengthened in Christ. I want you to know the author, Dr. Douglas Carr, is a friend and co-laborer I've walked with for over 20 years. I know him personally and professionally. I've utilized him as a personal adviser, strategist, counselor, and vice versa. We have ministered together in the nation, states, and cities. We have witnessed powerful signs and wonders as an apostolic-prophetic team, and he's one I trust implicitly. I value people who bring God to the table, look for God-strategies, and are not enamored with titles, fame, or fortune. I value the front-line frontier leaders who forcefully can advance God and His Kingdom and see the darkness that tries to consume us – bow down to the name of Jesus. Doug is one of those.

Every book Doug has written, God spoke to him to do it. His books are primers of truth. Reliable plumblines-built line upon line, precept upon the precept of truth that frees not only individuals but also lands and the people within them.

As I read 777 (Seven Curses, Seven Sprinklings, and Seven Blessings), I could not write a foreword without re-reading it in some areas up to three times! I have been caught up in God's presence and am being transformed physically and spiritually to another level of understanding and operation through this book. Doug covers the teachings of sevens in the scripture in the beginning, and I highly encourage all to take the time and let the Holy Spirit move over you as you digest truths we have heard. Still, God is taking us to another level of revelation that is extremely specific to the time we live in now.

The Body of Christ is undergoing a historical transformation that is critical personally but more so for our nation and world. This transformation is coming as the world has increasingly gotten darker, and the promise is that the light will get lighter even if we feel we are waiting for that in some areas. The way through is the same today as in 1776, the Civil War, or 9-11—through the Word of God, the power and authority of who He is in and through us.

Stop for one minute, and tell me which of these affected you, your thought processes, and your ability to be a light to the world around you. Since 2016, we have been facing COVID and all of its newly invented science methodologies; WEF/WHO, Klaus Schwab's intent to take over the world and eliminate nationally selected leaders; Bill Gates's desire to restructure farming and vaccinate the world; the 2020 election and now election insecurity; cultural shifts and identity crises that lead to highly antagonistic conversations we now avoid if possible; mass shootings; and border crisis' that have unleashed another level of government shifting our nation towards socialism.

That's enough right there, thank you very much. Then, add in your shifts. What did you experience? Who did you lose during COVID? Were your paradigms about the power of healing challenged during this time? How did those conversations go with God and other believers? How did you shift in your community? Do you go out less? Do you offer to pray for people less? Do you go to church regularly?

I lost six close friends due to COVID-19, had a minor cancer, almost died three times, and had a heart attack. Thankfully, the heart attack included an incredible face-to-face encounter with God, where He let me know everything I was about to undergo and what I needed to accomplish still here on earth. I could see the other side, and He told me it was not time to go there. He gave me what I needed to know; I have hope and a future, and He is leading me.

Before this, I had gone through a challenging season where life took a toll on me emotionally, physically, and mentally. I had given everything to the work I was a part of. I served, neglected the Sabbath for the sake of God's work, and saw the power of God gloriously. All the while, my heart was broken by numerous situations that were like endless shipwrecks I had to navigate for ten years. I could not discuss the situation, but God kept me and preserved my life.

Amid my navigating my world, like you, I've watched for the seasons of refreshment, of being renewed and restored. Thankfully, 777 is a powerful tool I could read, pray through, and experience. It was not just refreshing me; I felt my mind was sharper and stronger; I was seeing the world around me on a higher level of understanding and authority. I am under that transformation I was sharing with you, and I pray that he releases that for you as well. Bring it, Lord. Just release it now, even as we all take hold of this book and review and renew our minds. Let it be Romans 12:1-2 - transform us by the renewal of our mind!

We all need to guard our hearts, care for our lives, and steward what God has given us so we can accomplish all He has desired for us. 777 will take you through the season(s) you have walked through and transform darkness into light. God is going to do a work as you read.

I do not recommend this book just for individuals. Examine the material, the scriptural foundations, and the power of God moving through as you read this. Teachers, preachers, and workers of the Kingdom of God do what you need to do to get unentangled from every work of Satan, how he tried to pull you away from freely knowing the power of God and seeing God destroy the works of the enemy. He will do it for you and others.

Lastly, to you, be free. Let yourself find freedom as you read this book. In this world, I operate as a Deborah – it's just my nature. When God calls out the spiritual enemy and tells me what to say and do, I know things will happen and do. I noticed the other day, after reading the chapter about 'Taking back success through His hands,' a situation presented itself to me, and God said, 'Raise your hand to it.' I did, and immediately, I felt the power of God on a new level flowing through me and watched what was presenting itself as a danger – withdraw.

What is God going to do for you? I'm excited and hope you'll share your testimony with Dr. Carr.

Cindy Williams Moore
Michigan Apostolic Prophetic Coalition, Founder/Convener
Pray Michigan! & Call to the Wall, Founder/Leader
cindywilliamsmoore.com
Email: miapc@pm.me
Artist www.cindywilliamsartist.com

Preface

In 2016, The Lord spoke to my spirit as I was prayer walking one morning. "I want to show you how to help people transition from `Woe is Me to Wow is He' by teaching you how to teach others how to apply the blood Jesus shed in seven specific places to break seven specific curses and release seven specific blessings."

I began studying the seven places Jesus shed His blood. It was so interesting I began preaching on the subject. Later, I wrote the book *From Woe is Me to Wow is He!* Then God moved me to develop a seminar for local churches to help people begin the transition from woe to wow in a single day.

More importantly I began applying what God was teaching me to minister to myself and others. There are far more than seven curses, but in this book we zero in on seven specific curses Jesus shed His blood for.

In deep healing and deliverance ministry, we ask people to mark which of the ten curses they deal with as listed in the context of Deuteronomy 28:

a. Mental and/or emotional breakdown.
b. Repeated or chronic sicknesses, especially if hereditary.
c. Barrenness, multiple miscarriages, female problems.
d. Breakdown of marriage, family problems.
e. Ongoing financial problems.
f. Being "accident prone."
g. Suicides, unusual or untimely deaths?
h. Failure. Plans and projects meet with disaster.

i. Life traumas; going from one crisis to another.
j. Spiritually hindered in hearing God's voice, sensing His Presence, understanding God's Word, praying, or using spiritual gifts.

Each of the above is an indicator a curse may be operating due to personal, ancestral, or cultural sin. If we do not break these curses from ourselves, we pass them on to our children. The Bible says some curses are passed down ancestral lines for as many as ten generations.

Since God began teaching me these concepts, I have applied them while breaking curses off myself and others, and when ministering communion. The results have been extraordinary at times. I have ministered in the Branch County Jail since 1987, but the impact there has greatly increased as I've applied the truth of this book to the lives of these dear men and women Jesus shed His blood for.

In my case, when God dropped this idea into my spirit, I began ministering it. Now, after eight years of ministering the seven places with individuals and groups, God has highlighted so many new things to me, I was prompted to add the new insights He gave me through this much expanded and revised book. I give this book the new title: *7 7 7 Seven Curses ~ Seven Sprinklings ~ Seven Blessings*.

Immediately following the preface, I will explain the title and main focus of this book in chapter two, *Sprinkle Seven Times*. There are seven specific places where Jesus shed His blood so we can break curses and enter the fullness of God's intended blessings.

Introduction

I wrote *From Woe is Me to Wow is He* in 2016. Since then, these principles have become a living reality to me and for those we minister to. God has taught us to adapt the Woe to Wow principles as we break curses off countless individuals, we do public or private ministry with. God adds more insight each time we visit the seven places Jesus shed His blood to break curses and release blessings.

We developed a seven-hour seminar on this topic and minister it as often and in as many places as we can. It is also part of our Deliverance Ministers Equipping and Certification Program.

The greatest new discovery we now enjoy is how the Old Testament prophesied everything in this book before Jesus became the incarnate Son of God by coming to earth to shed His precious blood in seven places on our behalf.

The number seven is especially important in the Bible. www.biblestudy.org has a fascinating article, *Meaning of the Number 7 in the Bible – Bible Study*. I share part of it below.

> The Number 7 Used 735 times (54 times in the book of Revelation alone), the number 7 is the foundation of God's word. If we include with this count how many times 'sevenfold' (6) and 'seventh' (119) is used, our total jumps to 860 references.
>
> Seven is the number of completeness and perfection (both physical and spiritual). It derives much of its meaning from being tied directly to God's creation of all things.

According to some Jewish traditions, the creation of Adam occurred on September 26, 3760 B.C. (or the first day of Tishri, which is the seventh month on the Hebrew calendar). The word 'created' is used 7 times describing God's creative work (Genesis 1:1, 21, 27 three times; 2:3; 2:4). There are 7 days in a week and God's Sabbath is on the 7th day.

The Bible, as a whole, was originally divided into 7 major divisions. They are 1) the Law; 2) the Prophets; 3) the Writings, or Psalms; 4) the Gospels and Acts; 5) the General Epistles; 6) the Epistles of Paul; and 7) the book of Revelation. The total number of originally inspired books was forty-nine, or 7 x 7, demonstrating the absolute perfection of the Word of God.[1]

My wife and I read from the Bible out loud every morning. This year, Holy Spirit has highlighted the number of times the phrase "seven times" is used, including 31 times in the Old Testament and 3 times in the New Testament.

This is so significant; I will break them down categorically. The seven places Jesus shed His blood for us are not numbered "seven times," but later we will discuss each one of them. I assure you that you will see things that will add depth to your own study.

The New Testament is in the Old Testament, Concealed.
The Old Testament is in the New Testament, Revealed.

As we prepare to look at the seven places Jesus' blood was shed, you will see how the New Testament and Old Testament reveal God's eternal plan to remit sin and break curses through the shedding of blood. Now, I want to place the Scriptures where the phrase "seven times" is noted into several categories. I will italicize *"seven times"* for emphasis in each Scripture, beginning with one time when Elijah was wrestling for breakthrough.

Breakthrough: When Elijah and his servant were wrestling for breakthrough, it took seven times of going up before the breakthrough began to form in a cloud.

> And said to his servant, "Go up now, look toward the sea." So he went up and looked, and said, *"There is* nothing." And *seven times* he said, "Go again." 1 Kings 18:43.

Entreaty: In Genesis 32 the stage is set for Jacob, who had deceived Esau, to meet up again after Jacob fled from his brother's wrath to Haran where he worked for Laban and married his two daughters (Genesis 27 and 28). Twenty years later, in Genesis 33:3, Jacob wanted to flee Laban's cruelty and return home. He was fearful of Esau's reaction, so he entreated him by bowing to the ground seven times.

> Then he crossed over before them and bowed himself to the ground *seven times,* until he came near to his brother. Genesis 33:3.

Cleansing from sin: The first mention of shedding of blood for remission of sin is in the book of Genesis, it does not mention the sprinkling of blood seven times. But we know how God made tunics of skin for Adam and Eve and clothed them. The blood of an innocent animal was shed so Adam and Eve's sin and shame might be covered with tunics of skin (Genesis 3:21).

The first mention I find of sprinkling blood seven times before the Lord is in Leviticus 4:6, where blood was to be sprinkled whenever the people became aware of sinning intentionally. The following verses prophetically mention how Jesus would shed His blood seven specific times, in seven specific parts of His body, to break seven specific curses caused by human sinfulness.

Since there are ten references of this, I shall share all ten verses in their biblical order, beginning with the first mention noted in Leviticus 4:6. The law of first mention which www.gotquestions.org/law-of-first-mention.html introduces as:

> The law of first mention says that, to understand a particular word or doctrine, we must find the first place in Scripture that word or doctrine is revealed and study that passage.
>
> The reasoning is that the Bible's first mention of a concept is the simplest and clearest presentation; doctrines are then more fully developed on that foundation. So, to fully understand an important and complex theological concept, Bible students are advised to start with its "first mention."

📖 The priest shall dip his finger in the blood and sprinkle some of the blood *seven times* before the Lord, in front of the veil of the sanctuary. Leviticus 4:6.

This is the first picture of sprinkling blood seven times before the Lord in front of the veil of the sanctuary. In the Scripture, veils are literal coverings keeping people from witnessing the glory of God. The word "revelation," comes from a Greek word which literally means "unveiling." Jesus' blood was shed so the veil would be rent between God and those who seek Him.

This truth is explained in the New Testament by Paul who talks about the need to pull down veils. Unsaved people usually cannot hear God's voice unless we pull down the veil in order to call them to repentance. The Gospel is veiled for unsaved people. Second Corinthians 4:3–4 states the spiritual condition of an unsaved person makes it so they cannot see the light of the Gospel.

Remember that when you are witnessing—unsaved people **cannot** see. It isn't that they will not see but that they cannot see. They are blinded to the Gospel. Paul said, "And even if our gospel is veiled, it is veiled to those who are perishing. The god of this age has blinded the minds of unbelievers, so that they cannot see the light of the gospel of the glory of Christ, who is the image of God."

The veil that keeps lost people from seeing the light of the gospel is a literal covering—much like the skin covers the flesh and blood of our bodies. We cannot see what is inside because our skin veils it. The Greek word for veil is "Kalupto." You may understand that word better when you add the negative "apo" to it and have "apokalupto" which we get the word apocalypse from. The word that is translated "revelation" in the Bible is "apokalupto" and it literally stands for "unveiling."

The only real spiritual protection an unsaved person has comes as Believers apply the blood of Jesus and use it for spiritual warfare on behalf of the unsaved (2 Corinthians 4:3). (Adapted from my book *Free Indeed! Deliverance Ministry*.)

> Then the priest shall dip his finger in the blood and sprinkle it *seven times* before the Lord, in front of the veil. Leviticus 4:17.

This is similar to what we read in Leviticus 4:6, but verses 7–16 give specific instructions to be followed before the second sprinkling.

> He sprinkled some of it on the altar *seven times*, anointed the altar and all its utensils, and the laver and its base, to consecrate them. Leviticus 8:11.

Verse 11 reveals the need to cleanse the tabernacle and its furnishings before consecrating Aaron and his sons for ministry.

It is followed by a verse giving instruction for one who has been healed of leprosy. This symbolizes that salvation at the brazen altar (representing salvation) came first, then the laver, preparing for acts of service came second.

Before a priest entered the Holy Place of the temple, he washed his hands and feet in a laver (lavatory) of bronze.
(Leviticus 30:17–21).

📖 And he shall sprinkle it *seven times* on him who is to be cleansed from the leprosy, and shall pronounce him clean, and shall let the living bird loose in the open field.
Leviticus 14:7.

The next two verses mention sprinkling oil rather than blood, but since oil represents Holy Spirit, I include them.

📖 Then the priest shall dip his right finger in the oil that is in his left hand, and shall sprinkle some of the oil with his finger *seven times* before the Lord. Leviticus 14:16.

📖 Then the priest shall sprinkle with his right finger some of the oil that is in his left hand *seven times* before the Lord.
Leviticus 14:27.

As I was writing this, the Lord reminded me how I used to pray over every pew and anoint them with oil before Sunday morning worship. I began doing that again after writing this. It is making a positive difference the way we enter worship! My editor, Suzanne LeBlanc, gave a good suggestion here. I intend to begin anointing our sanctuary not only with oil, but also by faith, anoint it with the blood of Jesus.

The next verse gives instruction for anointing and cleansing a house where there had been sickness (leprosy).

📖 And he shall take the cedar wood, the hyssop, the scarlet, and the living bird, and dip them in the blood of the slain bird and in the running water, and sprinkle the house *seven times*. Leviticus 14:51.

Leviticus sixteen gives instruction for the Day of Atonement. It reveals how important it is to prepare when approaching the Holy Place, especially when there has been sin in the camp.

- 📖 He shall take some of the blood of the bull and sprinkle it with his finger on the mercy seat on the east side; and before the mercy seat he shall sprinkle some of the blood with his finger *seven times*. Leviticus 16:14.

- 📖 Then he shall sprinkle some of the blood on it with his finger *seven times*, cleanse it, and consecrate it from the uncleanness of the children of Israel. Leviticus 16:19.

Numbers 19 shows the priest sprinkling blood for those who have become personally or ceremonially unclean.

- 📖 And Eleazar the priest shall take some of its blood with his finger, and sprinkle some of its blood *seven times* directly in front of the tabernacle of meeting. Numbers 19:4.

Celebration and Restoration: The entire Bible demonstrates God's heart for restoration. I shared the pulpit at the jail recently. A young woman, Jessica, and I both were given twenty minutes to preach. Jessica's story beautifully illustrates the following verse.

- 📖 For a righteous *man* may fall *seven times* and rise again, But the wicked shall fall by calamity. Proverbs 24:16.

Jessica fell five times and was thrown in jail five times before she finally conquered her addiction but has been clean for nineteen years. She gave a great message—full of hope and grace for others who have fallen repeatedly. She encouraged those who needed to rise again.

Seven times is mentioned concerning the Year of Jubilee when debts are canceled, and people reclaim property they have lost.

> 📖 The Year of Jubilee. 'And you shall count seven sabbaths of years for yourself, *seven times* seven years; and the time of the seven sabbaths of years shall be to you forty-nine years. Leviticus 25:8.

Christ's sacrifice frees Believers from servitude to the law, but His blood also frees us to fulfill the intention of the Law.

Consecration: The altar, tabernacle of meeting, sanctuary, etc. were all consecrated to the Lord and cleansed for His use by sprinkling them with blood seven times.

A question was asked by a member of our writers mill. "Who cleaned up all this blood?" The Bible does not give a direct answer to this question, though a couple of passages may indicate it was drained away.

In 1 Kings 18:30–38, Elijah, during his confrontation with the prophets of Baal on Mount Carmel, repaired the altar of the Lord, which was in ruins. Then he dug a trench around it large enough to hold two seahs (approximately 24 pounds or 11 kilograms) which was filled with the water that was poured on the altar. We have here a trench built around an altar that received the water that ran down around the altar. That trench may have allowed the blood to drain away from the altar.

Ezekiel 43:13–17 may picture a cistern at the base of the altar which the blood drained into in order to keep the court clean from blood.

Thankfully, we don't have to worry about sanitation issues when we apply the blood Jesus shed. We administer the blood Jesus shed by faith!

 📖 He sprinkled some of it on the altar *seven times*, anointed the altar and all its utensils, and the laver and its base, to consecrate them. Leviticus 8:11.

Devotion: Regular times of prayer and praise help people stay in right spiritual alignment with God and man.

 📖 *Seven times* a day I praise You, Because of Your righteous judgments. Psalm 119:164.

Healing: The first mention of healing is also given in Leviticus concerning people who were cleansed of leprosy. Such cleansing is mentioned several times, as previously commented on in Leviticus 14:7, 16, and 27.

The phrase seven times was pivotal to the healing of Naaman under Elisha's ministry.

 📖 And Elisha sent a messenger to him, saying, "Go and wash in the Jordan *seven times*, and your flesh shall be restored to you, and *you shall* be clean." 2 Kings 5:10.

 📖 So he went down and dipped *seven times* in the Jordan, according to the saying of the man of God; and his flesh was restored like the flesh of a little child, and he was clean. 2 Kings 5:14.

Later, in chapter four, I explain the significance of Jesus' blood shed for healing through the thirty-nine stripes Jesus received through flogging.

Kairos Timing: Kairos means "appointed time." Seven times is also mentioned concerning seasons of judgment, beginning with the judgment Nebuchadnezzar brought upon himself in Daniel chapter four. I believe this also plays out during the seven-year tribulation.

📖 Let his heart be changed from *that of* a man, let him be given the heart of a beast, and let *seven times* pass over him.
Daniel 4:16. (Seven times refers to seven years.)

📖 "And inasmuch as the king saw a watcher, a holy one, coming down from heaven and saying, 'Chop down the tree and destroy it, but leave its stump and roots in the earth, *bound* with a band of iron and bronze in the tender grass of the field; let it be wet with the dew of heaven, and let him graze with the beasts of the field, till *seven times* pass over him';
Daniel 4:23.

📖 They shall drive you from men, your dwelling shall be with the beasts of the field, and they shall make you eat grass like oxen. They shall wet you with the dew of heaven, and *seven times* shall pass over you, till you know that the Most High rules in the kingdom of men, and gives it to whomever He chooses. Daniel 4:25.

📖 And they shall drive you from men, and your dwelling *shall be* with the beasts of the field. They shall make you eat grass like oxen; and *seven times* shall pass over you, until you know that the Most High rules in the kingdom of men, and gives it to whomever He chooses." Daniel 4:32.

Daniel mentions "seven weeks" plus sixty-two weeks.

📖 "Know therefore and understand, *that* from the going forth of the command to restore and build Jerusalem Until Messiah the Prince, *There shall be seven weeks* and *sixty-two weeks;* The street shall be built again, and the wall, Even in troublesome times. Daniel 9:25.

Punishment: In the following verses, God gives warning of seven times of punishment for those who refuse to obey Him.

- 'And after all this, if you do not obey Me, then I will punish you *seven times* more for your sins. Leviticus 26:18.

- 'Then, if you walk contrary to Me, and are not willing to obey Me, I will bring on you *seven times* more plagues, according to your sins. Leviticus 26:21.

- Then I also will walk contrary to you, and I will punish you yet *seven times* for your sins. Leviticus 26:24.

- then I also will walk contrary to you in fury; and I, even I, will chastise you *seven times* for your sins. Leviticus 26:28.

Purification: Numbers chapter 19 gives Laws of Purification concerning purifying people or things after any contact with unclean things.

- And Eleazar the priest shall take some of its blood with his finger, and sprinkle some of its blood *seven times* directly in front of the tabernacle of meeting. Numbers 19:4.

- The words of the Lord *are* pure words, *Like* silver tried in a furnace of earth, Purified *seven times*. Psalm 12:6.

Reconciliation: Then Peter came to Him and said, "Lord, how often shall my brother sin against me, and I forgive him? Up to *seven times*?" (Matthew 18:21.)

This is interesting because the Talmud required God's people to forgive their offender three times. Peter doubled the number and added one to it in an attempt to justify his readiness to forgive others. To Peter's amazement, Jesus extrapolated the need to forgive from three to Peter's seven, to unlimited forgiving as indicated with "seventy times seven."

- Jesus said to him, "I do not say to you, up to *seven times*, but up to seventy times seven. Matthew 18:22.
- And if he sins against you *seven times* in a day, and *seven times* in a day returns to you, saying, 'I repent,' you shall forgive him." Luke 17:4.

Resurrection: When Elisha raised the widow's son, the boy sneezed seven times before being raised from the dead.

- He returned and walked back and forth in the house, and again went up and stretched himself out on him; then the child sneezed *seven times*, and the child opened his eyes. 2 Kings 4:35

Victory: Seven times is also used to win victory and to celebrate it as Joshua and the nation of Israel experienced at Jericho.

- And seven priests shall bear seven trumpets of rams' horns before the ark. But the seventh day you shall march around the city *seven times*, and the priests shall blow the trumpets. Joshua 6:4
- But it came to pass on the seventh day that they rose early, about the dawning of the day, and marched around the city *seven times* in the same manner. On that day only they marched around the city *seven times*. Joshua 6:15.

Endnote:
[1]*Meaning of the Number 7 in the Bible – Bible Study.* www.biblestudy.org

CHAPTER ONE: AN INTERESTING KEY

There is an interesting key to victory given in Joshua 6:10 that many of us fail to use. Joshua knew how the complaining and negative, pessimistic talk of ten of the twelve spies to scope out the promised land. They observed the glorious bounty of the land but did not walk in faith. They focused on everything negative that might happen. Only Joshua and Caleb gave positive reports, and they were rewarded for it when they entered the land God promised. The ten negative spies died in the wilderness, because all they focused on was what might go wrong. Joshua and Caleb focused on God's promises and were the only ones who entered The Promised Land.

The key to victory I mentioned is the negative word fast initiated by Joshua.

> Now Joshua had commanded the people, saying, "**You shall not shout or make any noise with your voice, nor shall a word proceed out of your mouth**, until the day I say to you, 'Shout!' Then you shall shout."
> Joshua 6:10. (My emphasis)

This was genius! For six days the people were not allowed to make negative decrees. They were prohibited from speaking evil about their leadership, spewing negative thoughts, talk, and attitudes. The absence of negative speech prepared the people to make the positive shout that brought the walls of Jericho down!

I hope you notice how this underscores the importance of the phrase "seven times" in the context of applying the blood Jesus shed in seven specific places so we can break seven specific curses going all the way back to Adam and Eve, then release seven specific blessings by faith in the blood Jesus shed for our sakes.

Why do some Christians enjoy prosperous living and good health while others struggle continually with mental, emotional, physical, social, financial, and spiritual problems?

Is it because some people love Jesus more than others? Experience proves otherwise. Some Christians love Jesus with all their heart, soul, mind, and strength, yet struggle more with problems and circumstances, seemingly beyond their control, than others who barely give Jesus a second thought.

Do some escape ongoing frustrations and problems because they are better equipped and educated in the things of the Lord? That doesn't seem to be the case. While education and discipleship are wonderful, some of the best trained and educated Believers suffer as much or more than others who have little training or discipleship.

Is it the devil's fault who comes to steal, kill, and destroy? Yes, but Jesus came to give us abundant life. He does, however, leave us choice and responsibility in such matters. It is a mistake to blame God or the devil for things we bring on ourselves!

Absence of abundance in the lives of people who love Jesus, indicates the need to apply what Jesus did to their lives and intentionally break seven specific curses and invoke seven specific blessings.

Some people give into stinking thinking. They simply accept everything bad that happens. They may think they deserve life that is not abundant or free. They give into defeatist attitudes like: "I don't deserve to be financially secure, healthy, happy, loved, or successful." When such thinking is allowed to operate, the conscious mind may believe the Lord wants them to have abundant life, while the subconscious mind will sabotage it."

This underscores the need to be transformed by the renewing of our minds so we can be aligned with the Word of God rather than the thoughts of our subconscious minds (Romans 12:1–2).

We can and should break every curse, engage in every blessing, and come into agreement with God's truth that Jesus came to give us abundant lives.

This does not imply Kingdom people won't face difficulties. Paul said trials and tribulations are part of the Kingdom journey.

📖 Strengthening the souls of the disciples, exhorting them to continue in the faith, and saying, "We must through many tribulations enter the kingdom of God." Acts 14:22.

Although we may face tribulations as we advance in the Kingdom of God, Jesus calls us to break every curse and invoke every blessing He purchased for us through His blood.

In the Old Testament, there are lists of curses which come upon the disobedient and their descendants. There are lists of blessings too, for the obedient and their children. In the New Testament Jesus said, "If you love me, you will obey me." Loving obedience, however, does not make people exempt from curses until they *intentionally* break them through the blood of Jesus.

In one of my wife's messages, she mentioned the Old Testament, the New Testament, and the "Now Testament." She understands the Bible has thirty-nine Old and twenty-seven New Testament books. She recognizes, however, God is still speaking and bringing us into greater revelation of what is already written in the Word. She calls this increasing and ever renewed understanding of the Bible the "Now Testament."

Thank God for all the new books He has inspired to help us apply the principles of God's Word. Holy Spirit continues to inspire new books which are not part of the Canon of Scripture, any more than Bible Commentaries are. But they are inspired of God and deserve careful study, while holding the Bible as our highest source of revelation.

God has inspired authors to write on deliverance, healing, the Kingdom, and the like. Many of these books explain what God is doing *now* as He brings His people into greater understanding of what Jesus did, and what He wants Kingdom people to do. I hope He will even do so through my writing about Jesus' blood and its power to break curses and release blessings.

People must individually apply what Jesus did for the whole world, to enjoy His blessings personally. Jesus died on the cross for every person. God is not willing for any to perish. John the Baptist introduced Jesus saying, "Behold the Lamb of God who came to take away the sin of the world." Our Heavenly Father loves us so much He gave His only begotten Son that *whosoever* believes in Him will not perish but have everlasting life. Whosoever reveals one's need to personally apply what Jesus did by faith so they can enjoy the blessings He wants them to walk in. You can personalize "whosoever" by changing it to "You-so-ever."

Jesus took our sins upon Himself so we might receive Him, believe on His name and be born again. Since God so loved the world, and since "For he hath made him to be sin for us, who knew no sin; that we might be made the righteousness of God in him.," (2 Corinthians 5:21 KJV). Why are so many still lost and hell bound? Either they have not heard the good news, or they have heard it but have not personally applied what Jesus did to themselves by faith. Apart from the application of the works Jesus did, people cannot engage in the fullness of His redemption.

Jesus came to destroy the works of the devil, but James tells us to resist the devil and he will flee. If we do not resist, the devil does not flee, even though Jesus came to destroy the devil's works. We must *apply* what Jesus did through resisting, to enjoy the benefit of His work of deliverance.

One of the most frustrating things we face when witnessing is people who think they can be saved apart from believing in Jesus personally and receiving Him as Savior and Lord. Likewise, it is frustrating for those who minister deliverance when people think they can be delivered from demons without resisting them. It just "ain't so!" The Bible tells us to resist the devil and he will flee (James 4:7).

The same is true in breaking curses. It is disheartening to see people living under obvious curses and watch them give into them because they can quote how Jesus became a curse *for* us (Galatians 3:13). Yes, He did, but we need to *apply* what He did to enjoy it personally!

If a person does not engage with Jesus' sacrifice for his or her salvation by believing in and receiving Christ, that person remains lost, despite what Jesus did for him or her. If a person doesn't engage with Jesus by resisting demons, the demons remain even though Jesus gave us authority to cast them out. If a Christian does not apply what Jesus did to break curses and release blessings, that person remains under those curses and fails to enjoy all the blessings Jesus purchased for them.

Abiding in Jesus includes partnering with Him to work out our salvation with fear and trembling (Philippians 2:12–13). We are not pawns, moved here and there by God's hand. Jesus calls us to take His yoke and partner with Him. We are to forcibly advance the Kingdom, beginning in our own lives.

We partner with Jesus to inherit salvation. We partner with Him to cast out demons. We also need to partner with Jesus to break seven specific curses and inherit seven specific blessings. Jesus shed His blood in seven specific places to break seven specific curses and release corresponding blessings.

How I wish someone had taught me this when I began my Christian walk. I never even thought about the specific places Jesus shed His blood until I read Larry Huch's book *"The 7 Places Jesus Shed His Blood."*[1]

God changed my life through what I read in Larry's book over twenty years ago. The truths about Jesus breaking seven curses by shedding His blood in seven places has become part of my life and ministry. I continually apply the blood of Jesus to break curses, release God's blessings, and cast out demons assigned to keep people under specific curses. The seeds of what God planted in me through Larry Huch have germinated, grown, and are producing much fruit for the Kingdom.

Since Larry introduced me to this subject, I have studied it in the Bible and have read countless articles and sermons others have written on the seven places Jesus shed His blood. How I wish I could have discovered this before I went through the most woeful time in my own life.

My ignorance of the need to apply Jesus' work in breaking curses nearly destroyed me after 15 years of Christian living and 14 years of ministry. Even though I read through the Bible every year, I missed out on so much Jesus did for me simply because I lacked knowledge how to apply what I read. Hosea warns us of this danger.

> 📖 My people are destroyed for lack of knowledge. Because you have rejected knowledge, I also will reject you from being priest for Me; Because you have forgotten the law of your God, I also will forget your children. Hosea 4:6.

Lack of knowledge about Jesus' blood exposes us to curses we do not need to endure! Jesus' blood is more powerful than we can ever imagine. It goes beyond salvation, healing, and deliverance. Jesus' blood was also shed to break every curse. The word "saved" in the New Testament comes from the Greek word "sozo" which means "to make completely whole."

Jesus' blood was shed so we can be born again, regenerated, healed, delivered, prosperous, and set free to walk in His authority and power! He came to destroy the devil's work, "If the Son sets you free, you will be free indeed" (John 8:36).

We claim we are more than conquerors through Christ who loved us. So why do people of faith continue to struggle with their health, attitudes, finances, emotions, addictions, relationships, and the like?

Could it be we lack the knowledge of Jesus' blood which was shed in seven places so we might intentionally break the power of every curse over our lives? Have we or have we not overcome the devil by the blood of the lamb and the word of our testimony? We can win every personal battle through the blood of Jesus.

Barbara Yoder of Breakthrough Apostolic Ministries Network said we need to get back to the basics, including the blood of Jesus and its power to set captives free. Peter shares about the power of Jesus to deliver us from aimlessness.

📖 Knowing that you were not redeemed with corruptible things, like silver or gold, from your aimless conduct received by tradition from your fathers, but *with the precious blood of Christ*, as of a lamb without blemish and without spot.
1 Peter 1:18–19. (My emphasis)

The blood of Jesus was shed in seven places so we can resist the devil and make him flee. Jesus did His part. The same is true with breaking curses. Now we must apply His blood individually to break personal and ancestral curses and resist the devil.

I pray The Lord's Prayer nearly every day. I camp out on each phrase. For example, when I pray "our," I pray for my wife, myself, our five children, 24 grandchildren, plus many great grandchildren, and for the people in our church. When I pray "Father" I come against orphan spirits, rejection, and abandonment and pray to release of the Spirit of Adoption so each one will call out "Abba, Father." Jesus taught us how to pray, and we can identify seven places of power in the Lord's Prayer, which are: Relationship, Praise, Kingdom, Will, Provision, Forgiveness, and Deliverance from temptation and the evil one.

There were seven places of power and anointing in the Old Testament tabernacle, which housed the presence of God. Now *we are* the tabernacle of God. We have the presence of God with a new covenant—the sevenfold blood covenant. In Leviticus 16, people brought two goats to the tabernacle. One goat was for the atonement of sin. The second goat was to have the blood of the first goat placed on its head and then be released into the desert. Notice the word seven again:

📖 ¹⁴ He is to take some of the bull's blood and with his finger sprinkle it on the front of the atonement cover; then he shall sprinkle some of it with his finger *seven times* before the

atonement cover. ¹⁹ He shall sprinkle some of the blood on it with his finger *seven times* to cleanse it and to consecrate it from the uncleanness of the Israelites.
Leviticus 16:14, 19 NIV. (My emphasis)

Jesus' blood was shed seven times in seven different places! As we come to understand His blood was shed seven times, and in seven places with seven specific intents, we will learn to apply His blood to every area of curse and iniquity so we will know true "sozo"—complete wholeness in and through the blood! We will look at the first of those curses and blessings after we consider the phrase "no curse without a cause."

Curses always have a cause, often going as far back as Adam and Eve. In any case, whether the cause of a curse is personal or inherited, the curse is there until it is *deliberately* broken.

I wanted to use "engaging" in the sub-title, because we need to be intentional about going after the blessings Abba Father has for us in Christ Jesus. During one Daily Listening Room (where I sit and intentionally listen to the Lord and record what He says) however, the Lord changed the word from "engaging" to "invoking." I didn't understand at first, and "invoking" sounded religious to me, but I looked it up and now understand why God wants us to *break* curses and *invoke* blessings. "Invoke is a verb (used with an object), invoked, invoking.'"

Consider the definition of invoke:
1. to call for with earnest desire; make supplication or pray for:
2. to invoke God's mercy.
3. to call on (a deity, Muse, etc.), as in prayer or supplication.
4. to declare to be binding or in effect: to invoke the law; to invoke a veto.
5. to appeal to, as for confirmation.
6. to petition or call on for help or aid.

7. to call forth or upon (a spirit) by incantation.
8. to cause, call forth, or bring about.

As we consider curses and blessings it helps to understand how the first Adam, of "Adam and Eve" fame, brought curses upon humans which affect personal and ancestral health, character, prosperity, productivity, dominion, and fragmentation. In chapter two we will discuss how those curses have been reinforced from generation to generation.

The second Adam, Jesus Christ, redeemed for mankind the possibility for Christians to move back into blessing. We can "work out our salvation with fear and trembling" (Philippians 2:12) by applying what Jesus did when He shed His blood in seven specific places. Greater freedom and blessing will come to those who intentionally break each of the seven core curses and invoke each of the seven key blessings, which is the focus of this book.

Endnotes:
[1]Huch, Larry, *The 7 Places Jesus Shed His Blood*. Whitaker House, 2000, 2004.

For further study if you want to dig deeper: John 10:10; Deuteronomy 28:1-68; John 14:15, 23; 2 Peter 3:9; John 1:29, 3:16, 1:12; 2 Corinthians 5:21; 1 John 3:8; Galatians 3:13; James 4:7–8; John 15:4–6; Philippians 2:12; John 8:36; Romans 8:37; Revelation 12:10–11; John 1:14; Matthew 6:9–15; Luke 11:2–4.

CHAPTER TWO: SPRINKLE SEVEN TIMES

There are three major concepts in this book. The first is curses, which Jesus shed His blood to break. The second and most important is sprinklings, referring to ceremonial sprinklings of sacrificial blood that prophetically pointed to the sprinkling of Jesus' blood in seven specific places to empower us to enter the fulness God intends for us. The final is the access we have to blessings through the blood of Jesus. We will now take a look at "Sprinkle Seven Times" because it is key to breaking curses and the obtaining blessings.

The Hebrew language emphasizes letters and numbers in pictorial language. The number seven is incredibly significant in Scripture and appears over 700 times. From the seven days of creation to the "sevens" in revelation, Seven represents such concepts as completion and perfection, forgiveness and healing, and the fulfillment of promises and oaths.

The number seven speaks of completion and perfection. Genesis tells how God created the heavens and the earth in six days, and then rested on the seventh day. Therefore, the significance of the number seven is completion and perfection!

Jesus was "made perfect" by His work on the cross, that is, He completed the work he was sent to do through the seven places He shed His blood.

> So also Christ did not glorify Himself to become High Priest, but it was He who said to Him: "You are My Son, Today I

have begotten You." As He also says in another place: "You are a priest forever According to the order of Melchizedek;" who, in the days of His flesh, when He had offered up prayers and supplications, with vehement cries and tears to Him who was able to save Him from death, and was heard because of His godly fear, though He was a Son, yet He learned obedience by the things which He suffered. And having been perfected, He became the author of eternal salvation to all who obey Him. Hebrews 5:5–9.

What Jesus did for us on the cross and the events leading up to it are important, so are the statements He made from the cross.

Jesus' seven statements from the cross.

I give the central point of each one, then show the verse, and give a few comments for each.

Focus on Forgiveness: His prayer for His Murderers.

📖 Then Jesus said, "father, forgive them, for they do not know what they do." And they divided His garments and cast lots. Luke 23:34 a."

Jesus gave us a wonderful example of choosing to forgive people quickly! Jesus, fulfilling Isaiah 53:12, "He made intercession for the transgressors," prayed for and forgave those responsible for His tortuous death. I believe this includes every sinner whom He willingly gave His life for.

Focus on the Penitent. The prayers for those who repent.

📖 And Jesus said to him, "Assuredly, I say to you, today you will be with Me in Paradise." Luke 23:43.

Two men were crucified beside Jesus. They both joined the crowd in mocking Jesus. Luke, however, records how one changed his thinking about Jesus and asked Jesus to remember him when He came into His Kingdom. Jesus promised he would see him in Paradise. This shows Jesus' heart toward those who choose to repent late in life.

Focus on Providing for His mother.

 📖 When Jesus therefore saw His mother, and the disciple whom He loved standing by, He said to His mother, "Woman, behold your son!" Then He said to the disciple, "Behold your mother!" And from that hour that disciple took her to his own home. John 19:26–27.

It is very touching how Jesus demonstrated concern for His mother's wellbeing even while He was suffering His last agonizing moments.

Focus on His human agony.

 📖 And about the ninth hour Jesus cried out with a loud voice, saying, "Eli, Eli, lama sabachthani?" that is, "My God, My God, why have You forsaken Me?" Matthew 27:46

Even though Jesus understood it was for this hour He came, the pure inhuman torture caused Him to cry out in agony to His Father. Imagine being with the Father for eternity, walking in continue communion with Him until Jesus bore our sins upon His own body. His God nature knew the answer to His question, but His human nature released a sincere question at that moment. Suddenly, His human spirit, soul, and body blurted out the above question, "Why? ... " Can you imagine Jesus' Pain when the Father did not answer His question? Yet, by faith, Jesus said, "Father, into your hands I commit my spirit." With that He died, having paid the full price for our full redemption.

Focus on Completion.

 📖 So when Jesus had received the sour wine, he said, "it is

finished!" and bowing his head, he gave up his spirit. John 19:30.

I don't think it is within the scope of this book to do a word study on the word translated "finished" in this verse. Suffice it to say the Greek word "τετελέσται" - (tetelestai) means finished and completed to perfection.

Focus on His Father.

📖 And when Jesus had cried out with a loud voice, He said, "Father, 'into Your hands I commit My spirit.'" Having said this, He breathed His last. Luke 23:46.

Jesus' grouping of seven in the Lord's Prayer.

When the disciples asked how we should pray, Jesus gave a prayer containing seven petitions.
- hallowed be thy name.
- thy kingdom come.
- thy will be done on earth as it is in heaven.
- give us this day our daily bread.
- forgive us our trespasses, as we forgive those who trespass against us.
- lead us not into temptation.
- and deliver us from evil.

Jesus' grouping of seven as He described His Mission.

Look at how Jesus used metaphors to describe himself as the way, the truth, and the life.
- the bread of life (John 6:35).
- the light of the world (John 8:12).
- the gate to salvation (John 10:9).
- the good shepherd (John 10:11).
- the resurrection and the life (John 11:25–26).

- the way, the truth, and the life (John 14:6).
- and the vine (John 15:5).

Isaiah's Seven Spirits of Jesus. Isaiah 11:1–2.

- The Spirit of the Lord
- The Spirit of wisdom
- The Spirit of understanding
- The Spirit of counsel
- The Spirit of might
- The Spirit of knowledge
- The Spirit of the fear of the lord

Significance of Number 7: Exoneration and Healing.

- Every seventh year the Israelites were to cancel all the debts they had made to each other. Deuteronomy 15:1–2.
- Jesus described the fulness of forgiving to Peter by answering his question about how many times to forgive someone who sins against you. "Seventy times Seven." Matthew 18:21–22.
- Elisha told Naaman to bathe in the Jordan River seven times to receive healing from leprosy. 2 Kings 5:9–10.

Significance of Number 7: Fulfillment of Promises and Oaths.

The number seven also frequently accompanies the fulfillment of promises or oaths. In fact, the Hebrew word for swearing an oath (*shaba*) and the Hebrew word for seven (*sheba*) both derive from the Hebrew word meaning satisfaction or fullness. (sava)

In Genesis, God promises not to destroy the earth again with a flood and memorializes this covenant with the rainbow, which is comprised of seven colors (Genesis 9:8–15). Later in Genesis, we learn how Abraham swore an oath of ownership over a certain well of water (Genesis 21:22–31).

Abraham satisfied the oath with a gift of seven lambs and named the site of the oath "Beersheba," which means "Well of the oath," or "Well of seven."

The book of Joshua gives another example of seven's correlation with promises. The Lord promised Joshua He would bring down the walls of Jericho if Joshua and his army marched around the city once for six days and seven times on the seventh day with seven priests blowing seven trumpets. After Joshua followed the Lord's commands exactly, the walls of Jericho fell, just as the Lord had promised (Joshua 6:1–20).

Seven is also associated with promises in the Book of Revelation. in particular, we read of seven letters addressed to the seven churches (Revelation chapters 2, 3). In these letters, Christ assures each church community that if its members repent and live according to Jesus' instructions, each community will receive its promised reward.

Further, revelation often invokes the number seven in its discussion of God's promise to save those whose names are written in the book of life and condemn those whose names aren't not recorded there (Revelation 20:15, 21:27). The fulfillment of this divine promise is ushered in by groups of seven: seven seals, seven trumpets sounded by seven angels, and seven bowls of god's promised wrath carried by seven angels (Revelation chapters 6, 8, 11, 16).

The Significance of Number 7.

The Bible's extensive use of the number seven, along with such concepts as completion, exoneration, and fulfillment of promises, shows God ascribes a sacred nature to seven. Even though, not every mention of the number seven in scripture has a divine implication attached.

Since the phrase "seven times" is used 34 times in the King James Version, it is well worth looking at.

Fellow writer, Barry Gulliver, a member of the Writer's Group I'm part of, mentioned something with tears in his eyes when I told him about this book on the blood of Jesus. After a lifetime of participating in Holy Week observances, he finally realized,

Jesus did not shed His blood to get God off our backs, but to put us in the Father's lap.

CURSE WITHOUT A CAUSE?

Many lack understanding of how Believers can be affected by a curse. They quote verses like:

📖 Like a flitting sparrow, like a flying swallow, So *a curse without cause shall not alight.* Proverbs 26:2. (My emphasis)

The error of thinking "there is no cause for a curse because of personal holiness" is such thinking is too individualistic. People think "the cause" is totally personal. If they have received Christ and taken care of personal "curse-causers" they think they are exempt from any curse. Their life experience, however, often proves otherwise.

Let me illustrate. My wife and I live in Sturgis, Michigan, and lived on US 12 for over sixteen years. US 12 began as a Native American trail they traveled from Detroit to Chicago and back. Over time the trail became packed down and grew wider. It was called "The Sauk Trail."

Then migration began from the East to the Midwest. Settlers packed the trail down further with their horses and wagons. In the early twentieth century automobiles widened the path and deepened the footprint. Soon gravel was added, and logs were laid over soft and swampy areas and covered with gravel, making what was called "corduroy roads."

The name of the trail, now a major road, changed from The Sauk Trail to Chicago Road, then to US 112, and now is US 12. Semi-trucks and trailers soon began rushing between Detroit to Chicago with heavy loads. Pavement was added, lanes were widened, and US 12 was packed down with the footprint of several generations.

Each generation added to the iniquitous footprint of US 12 as well. Native Americans were driven down The Sauk Trail as they were forced to leave their land and lifestyle. There was ancestral worship, bootlegging, Al Capone, and his gang had several haunts along this road, including one across the road from where we lived. US 12 has been used for drug trafficking, sex trafficking, and many other sinful behaviors, all of which has left an imprint on the land.

Some may wonder, "what does this have to do with me?" Suppose the travelers along The Sauk Trail, now US 12, spread toxins as they traveled. Would modern travelers be exempt from arsenic or anthrax just because they didn't put it there? Of course not. So why would anyone think they are exempt from curses set in action "caused" by previous generations?

While confessing iniquitous patterns of our ancestors is biblical and helpful, we also need to address the curses caused by what our forefathers and others have done. Curses can be passed down for ten or more generations! As one generation after another walks the same trails of sin and iniquity, they reinforce the impact of curses sin brings upon future generations.

In this study, we will look at seven core curses which began with Adam and Eve's disobedience and have therefore impacted every generation since. Every generation since Adam's has walked similar paths and driven the "highway" of the seven core curses deeper and wider. The curses we face do, indeed, have a cause! Such is the bad news, but there is good news too. I love how Eugene Peterson sums this up in his paraphrase of the Bible, *The Message*.

> We follow this sequence in Scripture: The First Adam received life, the Last Adam is a life-giving Spirit. Physical life comes first, then spiritual—a firm base shaped from the earth, a final completion coming out of heaven. The First Man was made out of earth, and people since then are earthy; the Second Man was made out of heaven, and people now can be heavenly. In the same way that we've worked from our earthy origins, let's embrace our heavenly ends.
> 1 Corinthians 15:45–49. The Message.

Jesus is the second and last Adam. The good news is, the Gospel of Jesus Christ, shows how Jesus, the second Adam, shed His blood in seven specific places to break seven immensely powerful curses which have been passed down and have gained strength from generation to generation.

As each of the seven specific core curses is broken through Jesus' blood, seven specific key blessings can be received as we take back to ourselves the blessings Jesus purchased with His blood. Let us work together to apply everything Jesus did for us, not only for our generation but for our descendants also. In Jesus' Name and through the blood of our perfect Passover Lamb. Amen.

CHAPTER THREE: TALE OF TWO GARDENS
From Rebellion to Surrender!

There are two particularly important gardens in Scripture: the Garden of Eden and the Garden of Gethsemane. The Garden of Eden is first mentioned in Genesis 2:8 and is mentioned four other times in Genesis, as well as five other interesting mentions in Isaiah 28:13, Ezekiel 28:13, 31:9, 36:35, and Joel 2:3. I share of the most germane reverences below.

- So He drove out the man; and He placed cherubim at the east of the garden of Eden, and a flaming sword which turned every way, to guard the way to the tree of life. Genesis 3:24.

- For the Lord will comfort Zion, He will comfort all her waste places; He will make her wilderness like Eden, And her desert like the garden of the Lord; Joy and gladness will be found in it, Thanksgiving and the voice of melody. Isaiah 51:3.

The Lord God prepared the Garden of Eden for Adam and Eve. They were placed there, and first garden reveals human life as God intends it to be. The second garden is the Garden of Gethsemane which will be addressed later in this chapter.

- The Lord God planted a garden eastward in Eden, and there He put the man whom He had formed. And out of the ground the Lord God made every tree grow that is pleasant to the sight and good for food. The tree of life was also in the midst of the garden, and the tree of the knowledge of good and evil. Genesis 2:8–9.

Adam and Eve enjoyed the fullness of blessing as they communed with the Lord and each other in the Garden of Eden. They lived freely and abundantly, in total absence of curse. They were destined to live forever as they went about their business for God and ate from the Tree of Life.

We will look closer at the Tree of Life and the Tree of Knowledge of good and evil more in the addendum at the end of this book. Here we want to consider the full blessing and absence of curse Adam and Eve enjoyed before they sinned. They walked in unashamed transparency with each other and God. There was no rebellion, sin, shame, sickness, iniquity, poverty, natural disaster, or death in the garden. They communicated openly with God, each other, and even with animals. They walked in authority, power, and dominion over the earth.

Their only enemy was the devil, an intruder cast out of heaven to earth. He did his absolute best to find a way to steal authority, power, and dominion from humans. Somehow, he discerned it would be easier to deceive Eve first and then use her to draw Adam into rebellion.

The devil tempted Eve to reject God's sovereignty and lust after things God wanted to protect her from. The devil deceived her into thinking what she wanted was more important than what God wanted her to have. look at some familiar Scriptures.

- 📖 Now the serpent was more cunning than any beast of the field which the Lord God had made. And he said to the woman, "Has God indeed said, 'You shall not eat of every tree of the garden'?" And the woman said to the serpent, "We may eat the fruit of the trees of the garden; but of the fruit of the tree which *is* in the midst of the garden, God has said, 'You shall not eat it, nor shall you touch it, lest you die.'" Genesis 3:1–3.

Eve did not appear surprised when a serpent talked with her, but was oblivious the devil gained an opening when she listened to the devil's contrary voice through the serpent. His spirit was transferred to Eve because she didn't resist that voice. Even though she could quote God's command, the devil had her attention and was quick to divert her focus from God's Word.

> Then the serpent said to the woman, "You will not surely die. For God knows that in the day you eat of it your eyes will be opened, and you will be like God, knowing good and evil." Genesis 3:4–5.

Eve must have thought she could protect herself from deception. Satan crouched at her door, tempting her to think more highly of herself than she should. James outlines the progression from temptation to desire, from desire to sin, and from sin to death which follows the very same pattern as Eve's.

> But each one is tempted when he is drawn away by his own desires and enticed. Then, when desire has conceived, it gives birth to sin; and sin, when it is full-grown, brings forth death. James 1:14–15.

The word translated "full-grown" here is translated "is accomplished," in the New American Standard, "when it is finished," in the King James, and "having been completed," in the Biblos Interlinear Bible. It comes from the Greek Word "ἀποτελεσθεῖσα," used only here. It is Strong's Greek 658: To complete, accomplish, form fully, perfect, bring to maturity. From apo and teleo; to complete entirely, i.e. Consummate.

Remember when Jesus said, "It is finished!" in John 19:30? "Finished" comes from the Greek word telew (Strongs # G5055) showing how completely Jesus' finished work on the cross provides the cure for our sin when it is full-grown. Amazing!

The devil tempted Eve, and she became filled with desire contrary to God's will which gave birth to sin and led to death.

> So when the woman saw that the tree *was* good for food, that it *was* pleasant to the eyes, and a tree desirable to make *one* wise, she took of its fruit and ate. She also gave to her husband with her, and he ate. Genesis 3:6.

In the first garden, Eve was deceived, and Adam willingly went along with his wife. Perhaps Adam was more concerned with Eve's approval than God's. For the first time they put selfish desire before God's expressed will for their lives. They grabbed what they wanted instead of surrendering fully to God's command. They did not seek first God's Kingdom and His righteousness. They failed to trust Him to add all things unto them if they would simply put God first and trust and obey.

I meditated on this thought as I drove to the Branch County Jail to deliver a message on this subject. The thoughts flowed concerning how Eve and Adam chose to: look out for themselves, take care of themselves, protect themselves, please themselves, and put themselves as #1 and God as #2.

In the Garden of Eden, Adam took of the fruit and his actions basically said, "Not *thy* will, but *mine* be done." The blessing of obedience was lost at this point and the curse from disobedience fell upon humans. There are 10 major indicators of a curse resulting from disobedience given in passages like Deuteronomy 23:2–3 and 28:15–68. I give a very truncated list of these indicators below. Having any of these indicators in your family line, going back one to four or more generations may indicate you have lived under a generational curse of disobedience. I take this list from my Deep Healing and Deliverance Questionnaire I use for personal appointments.

Which of the following issues is part of your family's history in the last 4 generations? (Include adopted and blended family.)
- Mental and/or emotional breakdown?
- Repeated or chronic sicknesses, especially if hereditary?
- Barrenness, multiple miscarriages, female problems?
- Breakdown of marriage, family problems and alienation?
- Ongoing financial problems?
- Being "accident prone?"
- Suicides, unusual or untimely deaths?
- Failure: plans and projects meet with disaster?
- Life traumas; going from one crisis to another?
- Spiritually hindered in hearing God's voice, sensing His Presence, understanding God's Word, praying, or using spiritual gifts?

When I receive completed questionnaires from people seeking deep healing and deliverance, most of them have at least a few of these indicators, while others mark them all. I always share what percentage of the indicators are true of them and mention "that is the bad news, but there is good news too."

Jesus shed His blood to give us power to break every curse! Consider the curse Adam brought upon humans in the first Garden. He brought a curse of disobedience which has been passed down from generation to generation.

Thankfully, in another garden, the Garden of Gethsemane, Jesus, the "second Adam," sweat drops of blood that fell to the ground of that garden. When He shed that blood, He broke the power of the curse of disobedience in order to redeem the blessing of obedience for mankind. We can apply that blood and be free!

Larry Huch, in his excellent book *"The 7 Places Jesus Shed His Blood,"* first inspired my thinking along these lines. On page 26 of that book, he writes:

> This is how Jesus shed His blood in the Garden. Medical doctors confirm that at times of intense fear or agony, a person's blood vessels can literally break beneath the skin, and blood will begin to come out of his pores like sweat. Out of Jesus' pores came sweat and blood because of the anxiety or fear, and the turmoil He was experiencing. Why is this significant? We must keep in mind that we've been redeemed by the blood. The first Adam surrendered our willpower to Satan. The second Adam, Jesus, redeemed our willpower by saying "Father, not my will, but Thy will" and sweating great drops of blood. This is where we gain back our willpower to overcome the drug problems, the alcohol problems, the anger problems, and the depression problems.[1]

I spent a weekend musing over why people, including Believers, do what they know is contrary to God's Word and will. Why do Believers look at pornography? Why do they withhold their tithe? Why do they choose anger and hatred when they know God tells them to forgive? Why do they speak evil of leaders or gossip about one another? Why do they choose to do what they feel like doing rather than what God tells them do? I wrote the book *"God's Say So versus Man's Know So"*[2] because I see how many deliverance issues could be avoided if people would simply obey God rather than giving in to personal lusts. Bill Sudduth, past leader of the International Society of Deliverance ministers said, "There are two ways to get rid of demons, you can starve them out or cast them out." When we learn to simply live obedient lives, demons will not have much to feed on.

I believe God gave me a simple acrostic for the word "sin." I will give you the first word, then the third one, and later add the middle one which sums them all up.

Selfishness: Thinking it is all about ME.
Narcissism: Thinking primarily about self.

I turned to Wikipedia for the definition of narcissism.

> From Wikipedia, the free encyclopedia: Main article: History of narcissism: The term "narcissism" comes from the Greek myth of Νάρκισσος, or in Latin Narcissus, a handsome Greek youth who rejected according to Ovid the desperate advances of the nymph Echo. These advances eventually led Narcissus to fall in love with his own reflection in a pool of water. Unable to consummate his love, Narcissus "lay gazing enraptured into the pool, hour after hour," and finally changed into a flower that bears his name, the narcissus.[3]

Wikipedia also gives these traits and signs of narcissism. Our dimensions of narcissism as a personality variable have been delineated: leadership/authority, superiority/ arrogance, self-absorption/ self-admiration, and exploitativeness/ entitlement. Right in the middle of the acrostic "sin" is the letter around which all selfishness and narcissism reigns. More than any other letter it defines the reality of sin. The letter "I" stands for an independent "I" controlled life rather than a God controlled life. God showed it to me this way:

Selfishness: Thinking it is all about ME.
Independence: selfish independence, putting "I" first.
Narcissism: Thinking primarily about self.

In the Garden of Eden, Adam and Eve took things into their own hands. They chose to please self and each other rather than obey God.

Their choice caused them to have independent, narcissistic natures, commonly referred to as "the sinful nature." Since Adam, all have sinned and fallen short of the glory of God (Romans 3:23). This terrible curse affects every person until they break it by applying the blood of Jesus by faith.

Jesus shed His blood in seven specific places to break seven specific curses and release seven specific blessings. The first place he did so was the Garden of Gethsemane.

Jesus was tempted in all ways like we are, except He was without sin. He was tempted to protect Himself from the weight of the world's sin, His Father's judgment, and the penalty of sin which, I believe included spending an eternity in hell in the space of three days and three nights, which only Jesus could do.

Jesus usually referred to God as "Father," using two different Greek words translated "Father." (Pater which Jesus usually used, and Abba which He only used once.) Here he used a more generic term for God "Eli." It was on the cross when He cried out:

> And about the ninth hour Jesus cried out with a loud voice, saying, "Eli, Eli, lama sabachthani?" that is, "My God, My God, why have You forsaken Me?" Matthew 27:46.

Imagine the stress of the One who said, "I and the Father are one," knowing He would soon be separated from Father God. Jesus was tempted to be selfish, independent, and narcissistic. He was tempted to have a self-protective will.

Jesus asked His best friends to stay awake and pray with Him. He warned them to keep watching and praying so they might not fall into temptation, for their spirits were willing but their flesh was weak. Every one of His friends let Him down. Imagine Jesus' pain. To see the whole story, you can read about the Garden of Gethsemane from the three Gospel passages below.

📖 Then Jesus came with them to a place called Gethsemane, and said to the disciples, "Sit here while I go and pray over there." And He took with Him Peter and the two sons of Zebedee, and He began to be sorrowful and deeply distressed. Then He said to them, "My soul is exceedingly sorrowful, even to death. Stay here and watch with Me." He went a little farther and fell on His face, and prayed, saying, "O My Father, if it is possible, let this cup pass from Me; nevertheless, not as I will, but as You will." Then He came to the disciples and found them sleeping, and said to Peter, "What! Could you not watch with Me one hour? Watch and pray, lest you enter into temptation. The spirit indeed is willing, but the flesh is weak." Again, a second time, He went away and prayed, saying, "O My Father, if this cup cannot pass away from Me unless I drink it, Your will be done." And He came and found them asleep again, for their eyes were heavy. So He left them, went away again, and prayed the third time, saying the same words. Then He came to His disciples and said to them, "Are you still sleeping and resting? Behold, the hour is at hand, and the Son of Man is being betrayed into the hands of sinners. Matthew 26:36–45.

📖 Then they came to a place which was named Gethsemane; and He said to His disciples, "Sit here while I pray." And He took Peter, James, and John with Him, and He began to be troubled and deeply distressed. Then He said to them, "My soul is exceedingly sorrowful, even to death. Stay here and watch." He went a little farther, and fell on the ground, and prayed that if it were possible, the hour might pass from

Him. And He said, "Abba, Father, all things are possible for You. Take this cup away from Me; nevertheless, not what I will, but what You will." Then He came and found them sleeping, and said to Peter, "Simon, are you sleeping? Could you not watch one hour? Watch and pray, lest you enter into temptation. The spirit indeed is willing, but the flesh is weak." Again He went away and prayed, and spoke the same words. And when He returned, He found them asleep again, for their eyes were heavy; and they did not know what to answer Him. Then He came the third time and said to them, "Are you still sleeping and resting? It is enough! The hour has come; behold, the Son of Man is being betrayed into the hands of sinners. Mark 14:32–41.

Try to put yourself in the story as an observer as you read the following passage and witness the great struggle Jesus endured.

> Coming out, He went to the Mount of Olives, as He was accustomed, and His disciples also followed Him. When He came to the place, He said to them, "Pray that you may not enter into temptation." And He was withdrawn from them about a stone's throw, and He knelt down and prayed, saying, "Father, if it is Your will, *take this cup away from Me; nevertheless not My will, but Yours, be done.*" Then an angel appeared to Him from heaven, strengthening Him. And being in agony, He prayed more earnestly. *Then His sweat became like great drops of blood falling down to the ground.* Luke 22:39–44. (My emphasis)

I find it interesting the word "sweat" is used in only three verses in the Bible. The first is when God told the first Adam,

> "In the sweat of your face you shall eat bread Till you return to the ground, For out of it you were taken; For dust you are, And to dust you shall return." Genesis 3:19.

The second verse does not apply to what we are talking about because it refers to priests not clothing themselves with anything that causes sweat (Ezekiel 44:18). The third time is interesting and apropos because it refers to Jesus, the "second Adam," sweating blood in the Garden of Gethsemane.

The third time sweat is mentioned in the Bible was when Jesus' sweat was like drops of blood.

> And being in anguish, he prayed more earnestly, and *his sweat was like drops of blood* falling to the ground.
> Luke 22:44 NIV. (My emphasis)

Jesus shed His blood in the Garden of Gethsemane to break the power of the curse caused when Adam and Eve chose to be selfish, independent, narcissistic, and self-protective in the Garden of Eden.

Jesus knew what was going to happen to Him. His spirit and His flesh battled against each other, but He won the victory by submitting to the will of the Father. Jesus won the battle, broke the curse, redeemed us, and gave us back our willpower. He did His part; our part is to apply what He did by faith.

What Jesus did when he shed His blood in the Garden of Gethsemane makes it possible for us to break the curse and iniquity of "I centered" lives and totally change course from the "course of this world," as Paul mentions in Ephesians 2:2.

> In which you once walked according to the course of this world, according to the prince of the power of the air, the spirit who now works in the sons of disobedience.
> Ephesians 2:2.

Now, by the power of the blood Jesus sweat in Gethsemane, we can say "no" to the devil and fully surrender to God by saying "not my will but thine be done."

We can have our willpower restored! I appreciate support groups like Alcoholics Anonymous and Narcotics Anonymous but, according to what Jesus did in Gethsemane, we don't have to introduce ourselves saying "Hello, I am an alcoholic." Instead, we say, "Hello, Jesus won my freedom when he sweat drops of blood in Gethsemane. He broke the curse against my will power, and I can now say 'No' to drugs and alcohol—not my will, but His be done!'"

When we choose to break the curse of disobedience in our lives, the power of the blood of Jesus will strengthen us, set us free, and empower us to do God's will. When we apply the blood of Jesus and accept His grace, (which gives us the desire and power to do God's will) the curse of disobedience is broken, and our sovereign wills can be fully surrendered to Christ and be restored Hallelujah!

Many people, when hurt, build self-protective walls around their hearts. Countless people have been hurt or abused by others. They fear being hurt again and may even feel God has let them down. They tend to hold everyone, including Jesus, at a distance.

Thankfully, Jesus' sweat drops of blood not only made it possible to break the curse of a selfish and self-protective will, it also released a blessing of the possibility to restore our willpower to do God's perfect will. This is huge. This means dieters can curb their appetites! Addicts can overcome their addictions. People who know they should read the Bible, pray, and fellowship, will have the willpower to do so once they invoke the blessing of restored willpower. Paul spoke of this in Philippians 2:13.

I share it in a few translations so you can receive the fullness of hope it brings.

- 📖 For it is [not your strength, but it is] God who is effectively at work in you, *both to will* and *to work* [that is, strengthening, energizing, and creating in you the longing and the ability to fulfill your purpose] for His good pleasure.
  Philippians 2:13 AMP. (My emphasis)

- 📖 For it is God who works in you *to will and to act* in order to fulfill his good purpose. Philippians 2:13 NIV. (My emphasis)

- 📖 For it is God who works in you both *the willing and the working* according to [his] good pleasure.
  Philippians 2:13 Darby. (My emphasis)

- 📖 For it is God who works in you both *to will and to do* for His good pleasure. Philippians 2:13. (My emphasis)

Do you understand the promise of this blessing? Your will can be restored *to will* what God wills! Therefore, His commands are no longer burdensome (1 John 5:3). As Augustine reportedly said, "Love God, and do what you please." He wasn't advocating permissiveness, but expounding on the teaching of Jesus who uttered,

- 📖 If you [really] love Me, you will keep (obey) My commands.
  John 14:15. AMPC.

Jesus so loved the Father He fully surrendered His personal will in order to complete the Father's will through Gethsemane and Calvary. Jesus already did His part. It is time for us to partner with Him in doing our part.

Jesus overcame the temptation to be self-centered and to self-protect in Gethsemane. Only Dr. Luke, the physician who authored the books of Luke and Acts, mentions the sweat drops of blood. It is possible for humans, under great stress, to sweat blood; it is called Hematidrosis.

Hematidrosis (also called hermatohidrosis) is a very rare condition in which a human being sweats blood. It may occur when a person is suffering extreme levels of stress, for example, facing his or her own death.

According to Dr. Frederick Zugibe (Chief Medical Examiner of Rockland County, New York) it is well-known, and there have been many cases of it. The clinical term is "hermatohidrosis." "Around the sweat glands, there are multiple blood vessels in a net-like form." Under the pressure of great stress, the vessels constrict. Then as the anxiety passes "the blood vessels dilate to the point of rupture. The blood goes into the sweat glands." As the sweat glands are producing a lot of sweat, it pushes the blood to the surface—coming out as droplets of blood mixed with sweat.[4]

In the Garden of Eden, the first human sin of putting selfish will ahead of God's will and invoked a heavy curse against the world and all those in it. Adam sweat for the first time under the heavy burden of working land full of thorns and thistles. In the Garden of Gethsemane, on the other hand, Jesus surrendered all to the Father in the face of agonizing trauma which caused him to sweat drops of blood.

The blood Jesus sweat in Gethsemane has the power to break every curse of selfish, rebellious, or self-protective wills! As we apply His blood to break that curse, we can also invoke the blessing of restored willpower so we have the "will and the to do" Abba's perfect will.

The only time Jesus is recorded using the Greek word "Abba," which is translated "Father" is Mark 14:36. I wrongly wrote that

Jesus used "Abba" when He was hanging on the cross in my book *From Wow is Me to Wow I He!*" I was confused in my thinking that Jesus greatest struggle, necessitating His use of "Abba" was when He felt abandoned by God on the cross. I was wrong, it is used in Mark 14:36 as seen in in the best translations.

> And He said, "Abba, Father, all things are possible for You. Take this cup away from Me; nevertheless, not what I will, but what You will." Mark 14:36.

It is incorrect to say Abba is synonymous with "Father, which comes from the Greek word "Pateros." Abba does not mean "dad, daddy," or even "father." What it really means is "I will obey you."

I suggest invoking Abba, in the Name of Jesus, to break the first curse and release the first blessing. A helpful prayer is offered below to assist you in doing just that. It is important you pray in faith and not just hope. Believe God is doing what you ask for as you apply Jesus' blood personally. When you are done breaking curses and invoking blessings, there is a prayer to cast out demons that may have been empowered against you through the curse.

Each time you see the word "expel" at the end of a prayer or declaration, I encourage you to resist the devil and his demons by blowing, coughing or yawning so they will flee.

James 4:7 promises if we resist the devil he will flee! The best way I have found to resist the devil through prayers of deliverance is to cough, blow, or yawn in faith, knowing they must flee when you so resist.

Breaking the Curse and Invoking the Blessing:

- Abba, I declare I am redeemed by the blood of the Lamb from the hand of the enemy!

- Abba, I invoke You, in the Name of Jesus, to hear and answer my prayer this day.
- Dear Jesus, thank you for resisting the temptation to think about yourself or protect yourself in the Garden.
- Thank you for not throwing in the towel and falling asleep with your best friends.
- Thank you for breaking the curse of Selfishness, Independence, and Narcissism by saying "nevertheless not My will, but Yours, be done."
- Right now, Abba, I ask You to take the blood Jesus sweat in the Garden of Gethsemane and break the curse of a selfish, self-protective, and rebellious will from my life.
- I invoke Your blessing of absolute abandonment to Abba Father's will. I invoke the blessing of Your working in me both to will and to do Your perfect will.
- All to Jesus, I surrender, all to Him I freely give.
- Take my life and let it be, consecrated fully, Lord to Thee.
- Now, in the Name and through the blood of Jesus, I command every demon which was empowered by this curse against my will, to loose me right now.
- I cast you out and command you to go to the feet of Jesus Now! (Expel)

Endnotes:

[1] Larry Huch, *The 7 Places Jesus Shed His Blood*. Whitaker House, 2000, 2004, pg. 26.

[2] Douglas Carr, *God's Say So Versus Man's Know So*. Create Space, 2015.

[3] Wikipedia, the free encyclopedia.

[4] Source(s):http://en.wikipedia.org/wiki/Hematidrosis...
http://answers.google.com/answers/thread...

Chapter Four: Healing Through His Stripes
From Infirmity to Health!

Adam and Eve were created in the image of God by the hand of God. In His image, they were designed to live forever. The first Adam, however, brought a curse of death and disease upon the human race.

Jesus, the second Adam, came to redeem mankind from the curse of disease and death. Jesus has already redeemed those who believe on Him from spiritual death and will redeem the faithful from physical death. Paul wrote that the last enemy to be destroyed is death (1 Corinthians 15:26).

Isaiah 53 tells of Jesus' mission to redeem mankind from curses brought by Adam, including disease. Do you think there will be sickness in heaven? I don't. Jesus said, "For indeed, the Kingdom of God is within you" (Luke 17:21 b). Do you really believe sickness is a value in the Kingdom of God? If so, why do you think some Believers accept disease without resistance when they seek first the Kingdom of God here and now? It is unfortunate how some Christians, including wonderful servants of the Kingdom, suffer illness and disease and do not even resist it.

There are times when sickness is a direct result of sin. One example comes from the Israelites when they wandered in the desert. They had a "woe is me" attitude and blamed God for problems of their own making. We are often likewise tempted. Some people ignore their need to exercise but blame God for heart disease. Others eat sweets and carbohydrates like they are going out of style yet blame God for diabetes. The same can be said about smoking and lung disease, heavy drinking and kidney disease, or promiscuity and sexually transmitted disease.

The Israelites complained about their circumstances. They didn't like their food, lodging, leadership, or the water quality and quantity. Their complaints turned into blaming God for the situation of their own making. So, God sent fiery serpents among the people. As you read the Scripture below, I believe you will agree the people brought God's judgment upon themselves.

> Then they journeyed from Mount Hor by the Way of the Red Sea, to go around the land of Edom; and *the soul of the people became very discouraged* on the way. And the people spoke against God and against Moses: "Why have you brought us up out of Egypt to die in the wilderness? For there is no food and no water, and our soul loathes this worthless bread." So the Lord sent fiery serpents among the people, and they bit the people; and many of the people of Israel died.
> Numbers 21:4–6. (My emphasis)

Notice it was the **soul of the people** which became very discouraged. This was more than individual discouragement. It affected the soul of the corporate mass. Sin and wrong thinking often work like this; they discourage entire groups of people who are led astray and bound by discouragement or depression. These groups may consist of families, cultures, churches, denominations, and/or communities.

Years ago, the Lord arranged for me to meet various children of Holocaust survivors within a period of just a few weeks. Definite patterns soon became apparent as none of them felt they had a right to exist. Even though these children of Holocaust survivors did not all know each other, they shared unique patterns as a people group, including self-defeating behaviors. Their collective soul suffered and needed Jesus' healing.

Similar traits are seen in family lines where several generations put up with inherited physical problems from obesity to ovarian cancer, heart disease, and poor health from diabetes to diverticulosis and the like. Such diseases can become so normal in a family line that no one even resists them. They may complain and murmur about their problems but fail to take any physical or spiritual steps to solve their problems.

The Lord judged the Israelites for their corporate self-pity and murmuring. They said there was no food even though God gave them daily portions of mana. It wasn't that they didn't have anything to eat, but they loathed what they called "worthless bread." Rather than being grateful for God's provision, they grumbled. It was their own fault they wandered in the desert for forty years. God wanted to lead them into His promise for them, but their rebellion caused them to wander in the desert.

It is sad when people get stuck in ruts that cause generations to follow similar patterns of defeat, including family diseases. Such sinful thought patterns become cycles of sickness.

God's mercy is evident, however. Even though the Israelites sinned, and God released judgment through venomous snakes, God released forgiveness and healing when the people got honest with themselves and God and confessed their sin.

> 📖 Therefore the people came to Moses, and said, "We have sinned, for we have spoken against the Lord and against you; pray to the Lord that He take away the serpents from us." So Moses prayed for the people. Then the Lord said to Moses, *"Make a fiery serpent, and set it on a pole; and it shall be that everyone who is bitten, when he looks at it, shall live."* So Moses

made a bronze serpent, and put it on a pole; and so it was, if a serpent had bitten anyone, when he looked at the bronze serpent, he lived. Numbers 21:7–9. (My emphasis)

The people confessed their sin and when they did, the Lord provided a remedy for their sin *and* sickness. Some may think, "but that's Old Testament." In the New Testament, however, we discover the deeper meaning of the bronze snake which pointed to Jesus' death.

John chapter four illustrates the following truth, emphasized previously.

The New Testament is in the Old Testament concealed, and the Old Testament is in the New Testament revealed.

The Holy Spirit inspired John to use the concealed truth of Numbers 21 to reveal greater New Testament truth found in the Gospel of John.

📖 No one has ascended to heaven but He who came down from heaven, that is, the Son of Man who is in heaven. And *as Moses lifted up the serpent in the wilderness*, even so must *the Son of Man be lifted up*, that whoever believes in Him should not perish but have eternal life. John 3:13–15. (My emphasis)

Jesus' resurrection revealed the concealed truth of God's answer to sickness and death which came originally through Adam's disobedience.

Deuteronomy 28 outlines God's blessings upon the obedient and their children. It also lists corresponding illnesses, including the diseases of the Egyptians who worshiped false gods, which would come upon the disobedient and their children.

📖 If you do not carefully follow all the words of this law, which are written in this book, and do not revere this glorious and awesome name--the LORD your God--the LORD will send fearful plagues on you and your descendants, harsh and prolonged disasters, and severe and lingering illnesses. He will bring upon you all the diseases of Egypt that you dreaded, and they will cling to you. The LORD will also *bring on you every kind of sickness* and disaster not recorded in this Book of the Law, until you are destroyed. Deuteronomy 28:58–61 NIV. (My emphasis)

Whenever you see "LORD" in all capital letters, (in most translations) it refers to God the Father's proper name, "Jehovah" which means "I AM WHO I AM." This lends understanding as to why the Scribes and Pharisees were so enraged when Jesus used "I am" statements like "I am the bread of life."

Jehovah gave His only begotten Son as a perfect sacrifice to redeem us from all sin and every curse, including the curse of sickness, whether physical, mental, or emotional.

Visualize, if you can, Jesus' bleeding back. Picture His stripes, bruises, and bleeding. There is a healing evangelist who prays "by the stripes on Jesus' back, you are healed!" That's what the Bible says! Peter seems to misquote Isaiah because Isaiah says, "we *are* healed" Peter, on the other hand, wrote "by His stripes we *were* healed.

Compare the next two scriptures. Isaiah wrote:

- But He was wounded for our transgressions, He was bruised for our iniquities; The chastisement for our peace was upon Him, and by His stripes we *are* healed.
Isaiah 53:5. (My emphasis)

- Who Himself bore our sins in His own body on the tree, that we, having died to sins, might live for righteousness—by whose stripes you *were* healed. 1 Peter 2:24. (My emphasis)

All Scripture was inspired as people were "carried along by the Holy Spirit, we can ask Holy Spirit about seeming contradictions like "are" in Isaiah and "were" in First Peter.

When I asked Holy Spirit about this, He said, "Isaiah was looking forward to the cross by faith and wrote *"are* healed." Peter was looking back at the cross and was inspired to write "by his stripes you *were* healed."

We live on this side of the cross. Therefore, we can apply the blood Jesus shed so many years ago to our physical needs now for healing.

Years ago, The Lord dropped a phrase into my spirit, "I want to transform every *"Woe is Me" to "Wow is HE."*

I shared this concept with our congregation one Sunday and the following week people testified for 25 minutes how God had transitioned their "Woe is me" to "Wow is HE." Jesus already shed His blood for our healing. He did His part and now we need to do ours by applying His blood by faith to our needs. We need to diligently pursue the transition from *"Woe is me to Wow is He!"*

A pastor friend read this book and shared some concepts from it and encouraged his people to list their prayer requests on a "Woe is me" bulletin board and their answers to prayer on a "Wow Is He" bulletin board. Within weeks, the second board was full of definite answers to the prayer people had prayed in faith, including prayers for healing.

One Third of New Testament Healings included deliverance!

One third of the healings shared in the New Testament included deliverance. Jesus delivered a woman from a spirit of infirmity who had been crippled and bent over for 18 years (Luke 13:10–

13). A spirit of infirmity is a result of the curse, but Jesus shed His blood so every born-again believer can be redeemed from the curse! He cast a deaf and dumb spirit out of a boy who had several seizures (Mark 9:25).

Jesus paid the price for our healing through the blood which flowed from the stripes on His back. When Christians have sickness, the devil is trespassing, and we need to tell him to stop. We can *apply* what Jesus did to what the devil is trying to do, and make the devil stop!

As if to underscore what God wants me to share, I was tempted to give into sickness the night before I finished proofing this book the first time. Even though my wife and I have not had stomach flu for decades, I went to bed concerned for a friend who was suffering from the stomach flu. I had gone to bed before 9:00, exhausted from overdoing it for a few weeks. I woke at 10:45 pm feeling quite sick. I went into the bathroom feeling like I would feel better if only I gave into the sickness. Thankfully, the Holy Spirit reminded me to resist the temptation to be sick. Within a few minutes I felt fine, went back to bed, and slept nearly an hour longer than usual!

Jesus still heals; He still wants to heal! But healing comes through *applying* the blood from the stripes on His back by faith. His blood was shed so we can be redeemed from *every* sickness and disease.

I used to give myself an out when I prayed for personal healing or healing for others. I always finished my healing prayers with "If it is Your will." Thankfully, I now pray with greater expectation because I realize God is love, Jesus is the Great Physician, and healing is part of Jesus' Kingdom mandate and will. The Scriptures have many references to laying hands on the sick and anointing people with oil so they may be healed.

Though God may use sickness to discipline wayward children, it is hard to pray "Thy Kingdom come, Thy will be done, on earth as it is in heaven," and believe sickness is a value in the Kingdom of God.

2 Corinthians 7:8–10 does speak of a godly sorrow that leads to repentance. I do not believe God often causes sickness to discipline us, but some sickness comes as a result of the fruit of sin. Smokers may develop lung cancer and the tobacco should be blamed for this, not God. I have trouble buying into the thought it is God's will for His blood-bought children to continue suffering physically.

I failed to realize Jesus' work for healing was fully completed on the Cross. I used to end every prayer for healing with the words "if it be thy will," thus giving my faith an out in case healing didn't come. Healing seldom came and my family and I endured yearly bouts with the flu, colds, sinus problems and the like. Thankfully, since 1995, we have learned we have the right to resist sickness, just as we have the right to resist the devil. We no longer suffer all the sicknesses we used to suffer.

We used to get intestinal flu at least once a year, complete with high fever, vomiting, and the whole works. Now we resist it when we feel it trying to come. I have only vomited once since 1995 after we learned to spiritually resist sickness, and that was after a deliverance from Free Masonry. My wife didn't even have to experience that. Now we resist the spirit of infirmity when it tries to attack.

A spirit of infirmity is often present where there is a high fever. For years I carried an instant-read thermometer when I prayed for the sick, especially children. Time and again a child's fever would instantly drop from a high fever to normal after we rebuked the spirit of infirmity. But we didn't pray "if it is your will." Instead, we told the spirit of infirmity to go in Jesus' Name and through His blood!

Jesus was flogged mercilessly with a whip embedded with metal and bone. Jewish law allowed forty lashes, but they usually stopped at 39 because forty lashes often caused death. I've read there are 39 broad categories of disease. Others say there are 39 root causes of diseases. If either of those ideas are correct, then Jesus took one stripe for each category of disease. As I spent just a little time researching this idea, I found one web posting that said, "Yes, just recently in 2010 there was a reclassification from 17 to 39 broad categories!" What an awesome God we serve!"

That truly is an exciting idea—but I find another idea in the Scriptures more exciting. Matthew tells how Jesus healed all their sick. It doesn't matter if there are 17, 39, or 390 categories of disease. Jesus was and is The Great Physician and Healer! Healing was not limited to a few, but to all who were sick.

📖 Aware of this, Jesus withdrew from that place. Many followed him, and *he healed all their sick*. Matthew 12:15 NIV. (My emphasis)

I love the word "all" here. Someone said, "All means all and that's all 'all' means!" Do you believe Jesus still wants to heal "all the sick?" Some schools of Christianity teach Jesus doesn't heal today like He did while He was on earth. Many of these schools believe the Bible is the Word of God, so I cannot understand how they can teach contrary to what Scripture says.

📖 Jesus Christ is the same yesterday and today and forever. Hebrews 13:8 NIV.

Jesus healed yesterday and He heals today! His blood was already shed and by His stripes we were healed. All we must do is appropriate His blood! Jesus shed His blood in seven specific places to break seven specific curses and release specific blessings. We, however, need to apply what He did by breaking every curse by faith and invoking blessings.

Breaking the Curse and Invoking the Blessing:

- I declare I am redeemed by the blood of the Lamb from the hand of the enemy!
- In Jesus' Name I apply the blood from the stripes on Jesus' bleeding back to my health!
- I break the curse of sickness, disease, and "dis-ease" and command the spirit of infirmity to leave me now in Jesus' name. (Expel!)
- I break every ancestral curse of specific illnesses seen in my family line including . . . (mention specific chronic illnesses in your family line).
- Devil, I apply the blood from Jesus' stripes and command you to stop trespassing in my life! (Resist through blowing!)
- Jesus, I receive my healing by faith!
- Father, in the Mighty Name of Jesus and through the power of His blood, I invoke Your blessing that none of the diseases of the Egyptians will be upon me.
- I invoke Your blessing! I will prosper in all things even as my soul prospers, in Jesus' Name. Amen.
- I receive the blessing of good health.
- Now, in the Name and through the blood of Jesus, I command every demon which was empowered by this curse against my will, to loose me right now.
- I cast you out and command you to go to the feet of Jesus Now! (Expel!)

Chapter Five
Taking Back Freedom Through His Bruises
From Bondage to Freedom!

Why do you think people keep on doing negative things that hinder them from reaching their goals, hurt those they love, and give the enemy openings to steal, kill, and destroy? What is the underlying force which compels people to turn back to addictions, destroying relationships, causing pain, and bringing ongoing disappointment? Could it be there is an underlying pattern tugging at people to repeat destructive behaviors? Are there things working beneath the surface that sabotage our best plans and desires?

The first Adam and his wife were created without sin. They, however, gave into sin. This is when iniquity entered humans. I define iniquity as a bent, twisting, or distortion of character that passes down ancestrally. Adam and Eve's iniquity quickly grew in strength to the point one of their own sons killed his brother! Iniquitous patterns are passed down generationally. They are reinforced as individuals continue giving in to them.

Have you ever had a bruise or blood blister? Remember how badly it hurt? Have you banged your finger or stubbed your toe, and had a blood blister under a fingernail or toenail? These are called "subungual hematomas" and are more painful than open wounds. Small subungual hematomas usually require no treatment. However, the pressure generated by pooled blood under the nail can be extremely painful. To relieve the pain, a doctor may perform decompression, also called trephination, which allows the underlying blood to drain, relieving pressure and pain to the area.

Many people have spiritual and emotional "subungual hematomas." These require treatment by the Great Physician. Without His intervention the pain and pressure remain. I'm referring, of course, to deep inner pain people carry from iniquitous patterns, ancestral or personal wounds, trauma, heartache, etc. Such pain runs deep, often remains hidden, but the pain and pressure remain until Jesus is invited to do His healing work.

Physical bruising is evidence of inner bleeding. The blood flows beneath the surface of the skin. We already considered how Jesus sweat drops of blood to break the curse of a narcissistic and/or self-protective will. We studied how to break the curse of infirmity and walk in health through the stripes on Jesus' back. Now we turn to how Jesus' blood was shed through His bruising to free us from inner pain and curse of iniquity. Consider what Isaiah prophesied centuries before the incarnate Jesus dwelt among men.

> 📖 Surely He has borne our griefs and carried our sorrows; Yet we esteemed Him stricken, smitten by God, and afflicted. But He was wounded for our transgressions, *He was bruised for our iniquities*; The chastisement for our peace was upon Him, and by His stripes we are healed. All we like sheep have gone astray; We have turned, every one, to his own way; *And the Lord has laid on Him the iniquity of us all.*
> Isaiah 53:4–6. (My emphasis)

We need to take a deeper look at the word "iniquity." Jesus was bruised for our iniquities. The Lord Jehovah laid on Jesus the iniquity of us all. Unfortunately, many Bibles translate the

Hebrew word for iniquity as "sin" or "trespasses." Rather than doing a rewrite on this I take the following long quote from my book *"Getting to the Dirty Rotten Inner Core."*[1]

We understand that the sins of the parents are visited to the third and fourth generation, but we need to look a little deeper—the word translated "sin(s)" in many Bibles is more accurately translated iniquities ("avon" from the Hebrew) or faults ("paraptoma" from the Greek).

Iniquity defines the bent, perversity or pattern of ungodly or feckless and faithless behaviors like addictions, depression, entitlement thinking, anger, rage, promiscuity, victimization, and so many other negative behaviors and attitudes. Consider a well-known verse from Exodus.

According to the above definition I believe all will agree that rage and anger are ungodly behaviors. Consider a well-known verse from Exodus.

> 📖 Thou shalt not bow down thyself unto them, nor serve them, for I Jehovah thy God am a jealous God, *visiting the iniquity* of the fathers upon the children, upon the third and upon the fourth generation of them that hate me, and showing lovingkindness unto thousands of them that love me and keep my commandments. Exodus 20:5–6 ASV. (My emphasis)

Iniquity (avon): describes crookedness or perverseness; a moral distortion. It refers to the bent, perversity or pattern that affects generations and land.

**Iniquity describes character flaws
behind the action of sin.**

The Hebrew word is "avon" (pronounced "aww-vone) and is rightly translated "iniquity" 220 times in the King James Version. It is defined as:

1) Perversity, depravity, iniquity, guilt or punishment of iniquity
1a) iniquity
1b) guilt of iniquity, guilt (as great), guilt (of condition)
1c) consequence of or punishment for iniquity.[2]

"Avon'" comes from the word "avah" which is translated: iniquity 4, perverse 2, perversely 2, perverted 2, amiss 1, turn 1, crooked 1, bowed down 1, troubled 1, wickedly 1, and wrong 1. It is defined as:

1) to bend, twist, distort.
1a) (Niphal) to be bent, be bowed down, be twisted, be perverted.
1b) (Piel) to twist, distort.
1c) (Hiphil) to do perversely.
2) to commit iniquity, do wrong, pervert.
2a) (Qal) to do wrong, commit iniquity.[2]

> But we are all as an unclean [thing], and all our righteousnesses [are] as filthy rags; and we all do fade as a leaf; and our iniquities, *(Avon: bent, distortion, twisting or perversion)* like the wind, have taken us away. And [there is] none that calleth upon thy name, that stirreth up himself to take hold of thee: for thou hast hid thy face from us, and hast consumed us, because of our iniquities.
> Isaiah 64:6–7 KJV. (My emphasis)

The Hebrew word translated "filthy rags" refers to used menstrual cloths, which are a sign of infertility.

Have you heard people say somebody is a "chip off the old block?" Or "for better or worse, he is just like his father," or sayings like "like father, like son," "like mother, like daughter," etc.? When such statements are true in a negative sense, it is the work of generational iniquities or as it says in the Hebrew "avon." Avon's line of personal care products used to be advertised on television with sharp looking sales personal visiting and saying "Ding-dong, Avon Calling. Understanding the Hebrew meaning of "avon" brings a whole new meaning to meaning to iniquity.

When you visit a doctor the first thing they ask if for you to fill out a family history. Medical conditions in the family line set a pattern for the same in the descendants. In deep healing we do the same thing, but also focus on iniquitous patterns of behavior, or spiritual sickness, rather than merely physical conditions.

Praise the Lord! All is not lost! Jesus came to destroy every work of the devil! (1 John 3:8) He wants to break those generational patterns of iniquities and the power of generational curses—and He will—if we do it HIS way. But first, let's look at the Greek word that is best translated "faults" but often mistranslated "sins."

"Faults" is defined as: fall away, deviate from right path, fall under judgment and come under condemnation.

Let me share how New Testament Greek sheds light on this:

3895 parapipto par-ap-ip'-to} AV - fall away 1 = 1) to fall beside a person or thing, 2) to slip aside,
2a) to deviate from the right path, turn aside, wander
2b) to error
2c) to fall away (from the true faith): from worship of Jehovah.
From root "pipto":

AV - fall 69, fall down 19, light 1, fail 1; 90.
1) to descend from a higher place to a lower
1a) to fall (either from or upon)

1a1) to be thrust down
1b) metaph. to fall under judgment, came under condemnation
2) to descend from an erect to a prostrate position
2a1) to be prostrated, fall prostrate
2a2) of those overcome by terror or astonishment or grief or under the attack of an evil spirit or of falling dead suddenly
2a3) the dismemberment of a corpse by decay.[2]

I trust you have been patient while I have explained all this. The Bible gives specific instructions on being healed of generation curses and faults.

> 📖 Therefore confess your *sins* to each other and pray for each other so that you may be healed. The prayer of a righteous man is powerful and effective. James 5:16 NIV.
> (My emphasis)

A few versions in Bible Gateway translate the Greek correctly, in my opinion, as the King James Version does.

> 📖 Confess [your] *faults* one to another, and pray one for another, that ye may be healed. The effectual fervent prayer of a righteous man availeth much. James 5:16 KJV.
> (My emphasis)

James 5:16 tells us to go deep beneath the surface to deal with iniquity. It isn't enough to confess "I was mad at my spouse." We are encouraged to get to the root of the issue by confessing "I am an angry person," or "I really struggle with anger." We are to move beyond saying "I looked at pornography," and get to the root by saying "I am consumed with lust," or whatever the problem may be.

There is a curse working behind ongoing sinful patterns, especially when those patterns have flowed generationally. These patterns may include stinking thinking, depression, wrong responses to life, as well as addictions, promiscuity, covenant breaking, etc. As we confess our faults to one another, we can receive prayer from those who have overcome such faults and be healed!

Imagine what will happen as a person struggling with pornography or addiction confesses those faults and iniquities and receives prayer from someone who has overcome those things! Spiritual, emotional, and relational victory will be won when we break the curse of iniquity and receive prayer concerning personal faults. This is body-life as Jesus intended it to be!

So, let's consider how Jesus was bruised for our iniquities. When skin puffs up and turns purple or black and blue, it means the pain inflicted has caused bleeding underneath the skin. There are people all around us who are bruised, broken and bleeding on the inside. Outside they may act tough or paste on a smile, dress up nice and look invincible. Inside, however, there may be multiple fragments of hurting and wounded identities.

One of my greatest joys in ministering deep healing is when people invite Jesus to show them where He was and what He was doing when they went through horrible times of abuse or trauma. They often recognize Jesus was there either shielding them from further damage or bearing their shame and pain for them.

Recently a woman who, when she was a very young child, had been raped by her much older brother asked Jesus where He was when her brother did that to her. The Holy Spirit gave her a picture of Jesus entering her broken heart. As she recognized Jesus was there and realized his love and concern, she was able to receive healing for her inner brokenness.

Isaiah prophesied Jesus bore our griefs and carried our sorrows. He was wounded for our transgressions. But then, God speaking through Isaiah, goes deeper and states Jesus was bruised for our iniquities. Remember, "iniquities" refer to personal or generational patterns of perversity, shame, guilt, bent and/or twisted inner character.

Iniquity is much deeper than sin. Iniquities are the inherited character traits from which the actions of sin spring forth. Jesus was bruised for our iniquities. He bled beneath His skin to break the power of the curse of inner iniquity. Inner Iniquity often rules as fruit borne by inner pain and deep inner wounds. Jesus was bruised for our sake so we can overcome both the inner bruising, and the iniquitous character we have developed or inherited.

The bad news is we were all born with inherent iniquity. The good news is Jesus was bruised for our iniquity. Some of His precious blood flowed underneath the surface of His skin, hidden from sight, but powerful to break the curse of iniquity.

This is almost too wonderful to proclaim. Jesus paid it all, all to him I owe, sin had left a crimson stain, He washed it white as snow. Jesus' bruises provide healing for our pain from deep inner wounds and iniquity!

We know and sing truths of the Gospel, but they do not become personal reality until we intentionally apply the blood to break the curse of iniquity. The descendants of addicts are prone to addiction. The descendants of divorced parents or grandparents are prone to covenant breaking. The descendants of people who rely on government to supply all their needs are often given to entitlement thinking. The children and grandchildren of people who were sexually promiscuous or given to crime are often subject to similar iniquitous patterns. Such is the bad news of iniquity being passed down to the third and fourth generation.

The good news is the blood from Jesus' bruises is powerful and effective in breaking iniquitous patterns! Some of His precious blood flowed underneath the surface of His skin, hidden from sight, but powerful to break the curse of iniquity.

It helps to be specific in applying the blood from Jesus' bruises to explicit personal and generational iniquitous patterns. For example, if someone has always given in to a "poor me" spirit, apply the blood from Jesus' bruises to break the iniquitous pattern of the "poor me" spirit. The same applies to iniquitous patterns of anger, depression, bitterness, self-rejection, condemnation or any other bent or distortion of character leading to personal defeat. Once you break definite curses of iniquity you can prepare to invoke blessings.

Jesus not only shed his blood to break every curse and to set the captive free—He also died, was buried and rose from the dead to give us the Power of His Resurrection to walk out everything He did for us. Paul exhorts us to become like Jesus!

> 📖 I want to know Christ and the power of his resurrection and the fellowship of sharing in his sufferings, *becoming like him* in his death, and so, somehow, to attain to the resurrection from the dead. Philippians 3:10–11 NIV. (My emphasis)

I pray these thoughts will be engrafted in your soul over the next days and weeks. Holy Spirit will reveal one issue at a time until we are conformed to the image of Christ!

Before praying to break curses of iniquity and invoke blessings of holiness and victory, I challenge you to soak in The Holy Spirit for a few minutes and jot down specific personal or generational patterns of iniquity, perversity, shame, guilt, bent or twisted inner character so you can address them in the prayer after you finish writing your list.

Record personal and ancestral iniquities:

_____

_____

_____

_____

_____

_____

_____

_____

_____

_____

_____

_____

_____

_____

_____

Breaking Curses and Invoking Blessings:

- Jesus, I need You and Your bondage-breaking power.
- I declare I am redeemed from iniquity, by the blood of the Lamb, from the hand of the enemy!
- I put my faith in You and receive You as Savior, Lord, Deliverer, and Protector.
- In Jesus' Name I apply the blood from Your bruises to break every curse of iniquity, and bent or distortion of character from my life.
- I have specific areas of iniquity in my life and in the lives of my ancestors, so I now confess them one by one . . . (Confess from the preceding list.).
- Father God, I ask you to apply the blood from Jesus' bruises to break every curse of iniquity in my family line, including. . . (List specific iniquitous patterns.).
- Now, because of what Jesus for me, I invoke Your blessing of holiness and freedom from personal and generational iniquity from me and my children.
- I command every personal or ancestral demon working to keep me bound to iniquitous patterns to release me now in the Name and through the blood of Jesus. (Expel!)
- And, Father, since we are born again of the imperishable seed (Greek, "sperma") of the Word of God, we ask You to let us share Your DNA!
- In the powerful Name of Jesus Christ. Amen.

Endnotes:

[1] Carr, Douglas <u>Getting to the Dirty Rotten Inner Core</u>, Create Space 2014. Pages 18–22.

[2] Strong, James. S.T.D, LL.D. <u>Strong's Exhaustive Concordance of the Bible.</u> The Old-Time Gospel Hour Edition.

Chapter Six
Taking Hold of Prosperity Through His Thorns
From Poverty to Prosperity!

The Lord dropped some questions into my spirit while I was prayer-walking. I was meditating on Jesus' crown of thorns and God placed some things on my heart. I truly want everyone who reads this to receive this truth and live it out. I want you to prosper and be the head and not the tail. I want you to get out of debt, prepare a nest egg, and prosper. Here are the questions the Lord wants you to consider and answer:

- Do you want to be poor or prosperous?
- Do you want to barely make it, often paying late fees on your bills, or have enough money to pay all your bills on time, and money left over to liberally bless your family and others?
- Do you want to walk in blessing and abundance with the floodgates of heaven open over you; or are you OK letting the Devourer hold you back and corrupt or steal your wealth?
- Do you want to live by faith—grateful how God supplies all your needs according to His riches in Christ Jesus—or do you want to live by mooch—depending on the government or others to supply your basic needs?
- Do you want to leave an inheritance for your children, or leave them the burden of scraping up money for your final care?
- In short, do you want to break the curse of poverty over your life and invoke the blessing of prosperity?

I realize those who read this come from various circumstances. Some already walk in the blessing of prosperity. Others are retired and hope the money they put into Social Security and other investments will be enough. Some are disabled and unable to work. God's truths, however, apply to all people in all situations. Missionary Hudson Taylor reportedly said, "God's work, done God's way, will never lack God's supply." Such is true of individuals and ministries. Jesus became poor for our sakes so through His poverty we might become rich through Him. Do you really believe that?

> For you know the grace of our Lord Jesus Christ, that though he was rich, yet for your sake he became poor, *so that you through his poverty might become rich.*
> 2 Corinthians 8:9 NIV. (My emphasis)

In the fall of 2014, Pam and I downsized from a large house on nearly eleven acres to a small one on one acre. We obeyed some prophetic words which affirmed what we already sensed. We would become so busy we would lack the time needed to care for the home, property, and animals we had enjoyed for years.

We had an auction to liquidate the overabundance of possessions we had and still had to take over a dozen truckloads of clothing, housewares, etc. to donate to Good Will. It was quite painful going through the process of downsizing, even though we knew the Lord wanted us to. We had to "give a lot of things up."

Can you imagine how much Jesus had to downsize when He emptied Himself, left the glory of heaven, and came to earth to be born in a stable? I like the way the Amplified Bible elaborates this.

> For you are recognizing [more clearly] the grace of our Lord Jesus Christ [His astonishing kindness, His generosity, His

gracious favor], *that though He was rich, yet for your sake He became poor, so that by His poverty you might become rich* (abundantly blessed). 2 Corinthians 8:9 AMP. (My emphasis)

Let's dig deeper into Jesus' crown of thorns, and how to use His blood from the thorns to break the curse of poverty. We've all seen pictures and movies about the Passion Week of Jesus. We've seen the crown of thorns pressed into the skin around his forehead. But there is more to that story, and it starts back in the Garden of Eden.

> To Adam he said, "Because you listened to your wife and ate from the tree about which I commanded you, 'You must not eat of it,' "*Cursed is the ground because of you; through painful toil you will eat of it all the days of your life. It will produce thorns and thistles for you*, and you will eat the plants of the field. *By the sweat of your brow* you will eat your food until you return to the ground, since from it you were taken; for dust you are and to dust you will return."
> Genesis 3:17–19 NIV. (My emphasis)

God cursed the land in judgment of sin. Therefore, work became increasingly difficult. Work in itself is not a curse. Adam worked the garden before he fell. After Adam fell, however, God released the corresponding curse. As we will see later, the curse came against the ease, fruitfulness, and profitability of work. The curse on the woman's labor of childbirth robbed her of the joy and ease of bearing children.

Exodus 1:19 suggests the Hebrew women were vigorous and quickly delivered before the midwives arrived. I suggest expecting parents break the curse on a woman's labor and childbirth and restore the joy and ease of bearing children.

Recently a mother of three spoke of how difficult the labor was with the birth of her first child. It was so horrible she had second thoughts about whether to have more children. Thankfully, the Lord spoke to her about breaking Eve's curse concerning giving birth. This mother broke that curse, and her other children were born with very little pain or difficulty!

The Bible shows work as a blessing and an obligation. We are supposed to work hard, provide for ourselves and our families, and support the work of the Kingdom. Paul says people who are unwilling to work fail to live out their faith!

> *Anyone who does not provide for their relatives,* and especially for their own household, has denied the faith and *is worse than an unbeliever.* 1 Timothy 5:8 NIV. (My emphasis)

Part of our Christian duty is to work with our own hands and be as independent financially as we can be. While taking care of the poor and generosity are commended in the Bible, entitlement thinking is forbidden. Paul stresses godly independence.

> Yet we urge you, brothers and sisters, to do so more and more, and to make it your ambition to lead a quiet life: You should mind your own business and *work with your hands*, just as we told you, so that your daily life may win the respect of outsiders and *so that you will not be dependent on anybody.* 1 Thessalonians 4:10 b–12 NIV. (My emphasis)

There were people in Thessalonica who felt they were entitled to take advantage of the generosity of others rather than earning their own keep, just as there is nowadays.

> For even when we were with you, we gave you this rule: *"The one who is unwilling to work shall not eat."* We hear that some among you are idle and disruptive. They are not busy; they

are busybodies. Such people we command and urge in the Lord Jesus Christ to *settle down and earn the food they eat.* 2 Thessalonians 3:10–12 NIV. (My emphasis)

I heard a true story of an older woman whose adult son still lived with her. The woman worked extremely hard, but her son seldom held down a job for more than a few weeks. Even though she was well past retirement age, she wouldn't even consider quitting her job because she wouldn't receive enough retirement benefits to take care of her and her son. Her friends tried to convince her she should retire and let her son learn to get a job and earn his keep.

God finally used this woman's waning strength to convince her it was time to retire. The next day when her son woke up, he noticed his mother was still home. He yelled at her, saying, "Mom, you are going to be late for work," to which she replied, "I finally retired, I am not going to work." He couldn't believe it, but the next day she was still at home, so he asked, "How are we going to have money for groceries and rent?" She said, "I don't know, I trust the Lord will take care of me, but I don't know about you."

After a few days of wondering how his mother would be able to take care of their needs without working, the son decided to do something about it. He was gone the next day when his mother woke up and didn't return home until late in the day. His mother asked him where he had been all day and he replied, "I went to look for a job and I start tomorrow!" Moral of the story: there are times when parents must stop forking over money, housing, and provision to motivate their adult children to take care of themselves.

Our church was led to have a "Basket of Abundance" one year. It was a big basket with a set of ceramic hands in the bottom which represented God's hands. Our people are generous and made offerings to the basket and we allowed people to take money from it to meet urgent needs like medical bills, avoid utility shutoffs, help them pay their rent, buy food, etc.

A lovely young couple with an infant child began attending our church. As we ministered to them their very first Sunday, we found they were about to be evicted from their home because they didn't have the money to pay the rent. We gladly let them take from the basket of abundance to meet their need.

They continued to dip into the basket a couple of times a month for money for groceries, etc. A month later they were about to evicted again, so we let them take money for rent. It became apparent they would rather let others help pay their bills than find a job, and they depleted the Basket of Abundance.

When their next rent was due, they called and asked to meet with me, hoping for another handout. My wife and I agreed to meet with them, and I explained what the Bible says about the responsibility to take care of one's own family. I asked the young man if he would take a job if I could help him find one. He said he would, and I offered to loan him the money for the current month's rent if he would go to work and pay me back by giving me 10% of each paycheck. He said yes and we drew up a contract, signed it, and we loaned them the rent money.

I called my oldest son, Eric, who is a hard-working contractor. He agreed to hire the man for a fair wage. The man did show up for work at 6:00 a.m. the next day, but failed to show for work the following day, so I called him, and he said the work was too hard. He finally paid back his loan when they got their tax return, but they continued to live off mooch. I tried to make it clear that he had a full-time job already. His job was to leave every morning and go from business to business, applying for a job until he got one! I told him to find *a* job right away and quit waiting for *the* job he wanted.

They quit coming to church after their "free lunch" dried up, but he came back a few months later saying he was called to be a missionary and wondered if we would support him. I told him, "Absolutely not!" Jesus taught "He who is responsible in that which is least will be given more, but he who is not responsible in that which is least, even what he has will be taken away and given to another" (See Luke 16:10 for example.).

This man's first responsibility was to take care of his wife and son, and until he was faithful in that, it would be a mistake to support him in ministry.

Christians should be the best, most reliable, and productive workers regardless of their career. Laziness is not a Kingdom value. When Believers work harder and with better attitudes than others, they will receive inheritance from the Lord. Believers are called to work at whatever job they have as serving the Lord.

> Whatever you do, work at it with all your heart, as working for the Lord, not for human masters, since you know that *you will receive an inheritance from the Lord* as a reward. *It is the Lord Christ you are serving.* Colossians 3:23–24 NIV.
> (My emphasis)

Work is not a curse, but there is a curse against the ease of work, productivity, and prosperity which entered through Adam's fall. God cursed the ground with thorns and thistles. Adam still tended his crops but now had to till and cultivate by the sweat of his brow. He had to work increasingly harder to earn less. There were thorns and thistles to contend with. To the Jewish people the thorn bush became a symbol for the curse of poverty.

The curse against Adam's work in Genesis 3:17–19 immediately made his work harder. He had to put forth greater effort for less increase. Evidently, he began to sweat for the first time.

It is interesting the word "sweat" is first mentioned soon after Adam sinned and God warned him, "In the sweat of your face you shall eat bread Till you return to the ground, For out of it you were taken; For dust you *are,* And to dust you shall return." (Genesis 3:19)

Everything grew more difficult for Adam after the curse. The last verse using the word "sweat" is interesting because it refers to Jesus, whom the Bible refers to as the "second Adam."

> And being in anguish, he prayed more earnestly, and *his sweat was like drops of blood falling to the ground.*
> Luke 22:44 NIV. (My emphasis)

Jesus expands the thought of how the curse of poverty works to spiritual poverty in the Parable of the Sower (Matthew 13, Mark 4, Luke 8). A parable is an earthly story with a heavenly meaning. Consider how Mark shares the heavenly meaning of the good seed of the Gospel which was sown among thorns.

> Now these are the ones sown among *thorns;* they are the ones who hear the word, and the cares of this world, the deceitfulness of riches, and the desires for other things *entering in choke the word, and **it** becomes unfruitful.*
> Mark 4:18–19. (My emphasis)

The word "it" in Mark 4:18 refers to the good word of the Gospel which is sown into humans. The Gospel seed becomes unfruitful in the lives of people caught up in the cares of this world and the deceitfulness of riches! The unfruitfulness caused by the cares of this world, the deceitfulness of riches, and desires for other things of no more value than thorns and thistles in the Kingdom of God.

When we worry about money, housing, food, and clothing, it shows we are trusting ourselves or others rather than the Lord. Jesus calls us to do the opposite.

> But seek first the kingdom of God and His righteousness, and all these things shall be added to you. Matthew 6:33.

If you read the context of Matthew 6:33, you will see it tells us to trust God with our needs, but it does not relieve us from the responsibility of doing what God tells us to do. Seeking God's Kingdom means seeking the rein of Christ in our lives, which includes receiving His imputed righteousness by faith. Righteousness also means being in the right place, at the right time, with the right people, doing the right things! Part of seeking first the Kingdom of God and his righteousness is seeking a good job where you can work, witness, and receive income to bless you, your family, and Kingdom endeavors.

There may be a curse of poverty at work when healthy people are unable to find or keep a good job. Considering the curse of poverty symbolized by thorns and thistles, it is interesting how Matthew sums up the blessing of seed sown into good Kingdom soil.

> But the seed falling on good soil refers to someone who hears the word and understands it. This is the one who produces a crop, yielding a hundred, sixty or thirty times what was sown." Matthew 13:23 NIV.

Let's take this all back to the blood Jesus shed from when the thorns and thistles of Adam's curse became His mocking crown. Jesus, the Son of God, wore the crown of thorns. On behalf of sinners, He allowed Himself to be stripped naked and hung on the Cross, cursed by God. I love something written in an article by Jud Davis on the Internet. He says:

> "The story of the Bible is this. Adam comes naked to a live tree and spiritually murders the entire human race by a single act of disobedience. Jesus comes to a dead tree and allows Himself to be stripped naked. Then, in the ultimate act of obedience—His very death after a lifetime of full and total obedience to God—He makes alive all those who would ever by God's grace repent of their sins and trust in Him alone for salvation."[1]

Jesus totally emptied himself. He became poor for our sakes. He willingly became subject to public humiliation in order to break the power of shame off those who will follow Him. Try to visualize what Jesus went through before He ever made it to the cross. Imagine yourself as part of the crowd standing by as Jesus went through what we call "The Passion."

Picture going through what Jesus did. Imagine being stripped in public, then having a king's robe forced over you. Envision having a thorny crown pushed into your skin. Picture the mocking worship and being spit upon. Visualize having a staff forced into your hand and then yanked from your hand and being beaten on the head repeatedly with it. Jesus was a bloody mess and traumatized with abuse before his hands were ever nailed to the cross.

> 📖 Then the governor's soldiers took Jesus into the Praetorium and gathered the whole company of soldiers around him. *They stripped him* and *put a scarlet robe on him,* and then *twisted together a crown of thorns and set it on his head.* They put a staff in his right hand. Then they knelt in front of him and mocked him. "Hail, king of the Jews!" they said. *They spit on him, and took the staff and struck him on the head again and again.*
> Matthew 27:27–30 NIV. (My emphasis)

Jesus wore a crown of thorns, representing the curse of poverty, on His head. I've had my head poked with thorns when cutting wood or pushing through brambles. Thorn pokes are extremely painful. They turn red and hurt for days.

Jesus had a whole crown of thorns placed on His head. He willingly bore the crown of thorns to break Adam's curse of poverty! Therefore, we have a blood covenant with Him, and through Him, to work and make good money, to break curses of poverty and mental poverty, and to make the devil give back our money! We must apply it by faith to enjoy it—just like salvation. Jesus died that all might be saved, but it takes an act of faith in receiving these blessings to have them.

The spirits of mental poverty plot to keep you poor through twisted mindsets concerning wealth. When people cannot get out of financial problems, regardless of how much money they make, demons of mental poverty may be at work. They short circuit your thinking about making money, spending money, giving, investing, and anything else which brings increase.

I remember a dear family in one church I pastored long before I understood how curses of poverty and spirits of mental poverty worked. They received a good-sized inheritance which could have paid off all their bills, helped them make a down payment on a decent home, and increase their standard of living. But their thinking was off, so the money ran through their fingers like water. Like many who win lotteries or receive large settlements, they were in worse shape a few years later than they were before their great blessing of wealth.

The curse of poverty makes everything harder. Before God cursed the ground, Adam was blessed. God blessed his work, and it yielded great abundance. But when the curse came, the ground which once yielded abundance was cursed and Adam had to work harder and harder to barely get by.

I personally lived under the curse of poverty. Many faithful Believers still live there, existing paycheck to paycheck. I lived paycheck to paycheck even when I received regular paychecks, rather than pay based on the willingness and ability of a small congregation to meet our church budget.

The devil wants to hold us under a curse of poverty. God wants us to be so blessed we can leave an inheritance to our grandchildren.

> 📖 A good man *leaves an inheritance* for his children's children, but a sinner's wealth is stored up for the righteous.
> Proverbs 13:22 NIV. (My emphasis)

I cannot and do not believe God wants us to live as paupers and stick our children with the burden of paying for our funerals. God not only wants us to have enough for ourselves but also an inheritance to leave our children and grandchildren.

I know a wonderful couple who inherited enough money from their parents to pay cash for a house! Both the man and his sister inherited the same amount. His parents were not rich, but they built a sizable inheritance to pass on. God wants to release such favor through us to our children!

Even though Jesus became poor for our sakes, He always had enough for himself and for others in need. He became poor when He left the splendor of heaven, but He always had all the food and clothing he needed. Once, when He needed money to pay taxes, God had a fish waiting with a gold coin in its mouth to take care of that bill. I jokingly say I tried that before my taxes were due and wasn't even able to catch a fish! The point is: Jesus was never in want. Do you think He wants any of us to be in want? Doesn't He promise to supply all our needs?

The Church is called to help those who cannot help themselves, including the disabled, orphans, widows, and the disadvantaged. Still, the New Testament says those who can take care of their families are responsible to do so. Larry Huch wrote "that if people are able to work and are not working, they are living by mooch, not by faith!"[2]

Living by faith includes working for a living, believing that God will bless your labor!

We have been redeemed from the curse of poverty through the blood of the Lamb. Jesus took the curse of thorns, shed His blood and broke that curse of poverty. Now, if we will appropriate what He has done—we too can walk in the blessing of provision God wants to release to us, for us and even for our children.

Remember the questions I asked at the beginning of this chapter? The first one was "Do you want to be poor or prosperous?" We have a choice in the matter. Jesus shed His blood to break the curse of poverty when He wore the crown of thorns. When we apply that blood, by faith, we can break personal and ancestral curses of poverty and invoke the blessing of prosperity.

Breaking the Curse and Invoking the Blessing:

- I am redeemed by the blood of the Lamb from the hand of the enemy and from poverty.
- In Jesus' Name I apply the drops from Jesus' bleeding brow to win back my prosperity!
- I break every curse of poverty and command the spirit of mental poverty to leave me now. (Expel!)
- Jesus became poor for my sake so I may be rich through Him.
- I now invoke God's blessing of riches through Christ.

✝ Father, help me work hard, and produce wealth to bless my family and Your Kingdom.
✝ Devil, give me back my money!
✝ In Jesus' Name, amen.

ADDENDUM ON PROSPERITY

I did not teach about tithing in the previous chapter, even though tithing is a prerequisite to God rebuking the devourer (Malachi 3:6–12). I do want to mention some things God has taught us about sowing financial seed into good soil. Pam and I attended a conference in the fall of 2015. Our gross pay for the week was $180.00. Our hotel for the weekend was more than our paycheck. We had little extra to give and were thankful for the $1.00 menu at McDonalds.

A minister friend noticed we didn't have money to sow and slipped some cash into our hands. I'm not sure how much he put in my hand, but it was a $20.00 bill with another bill folded inside. We put that in the offering. Holy Spirit began working on me, so during the next offering I emptied my pockets and sowed into that good soil, the rest of the money I had. We have increased our sowing since then and listen to what is happening!

A few of the blessings we've received in the next few months included:

$750.00 in unexpected and unsolicited tithes to our church from woman in California. Two "blessing tithes" to me from a woman in Kalamazoo adding up to nearly $400.00. She says she gets "unexpected financial blessings" in the tune of thousands of dollars to date, and often she does something special for me and Freedom Ministries.

The day before I finished this chapter, our church received a tithe of $500.00 with a promise of the same each month until this woman from the east side of our state found a new church. Since we sowed the good seed, we also received a $60.00 blessing to me from a pastor in Kalamazoo. Another church in Kalamazoo began sowing $50.00 per month into Doug Carr Freedom Ministries.

Just before I sent a new syllabus to the printer, I received a $250.00 tithe from a prayer ministry in Grand Rapids which paid over half of the cost of our newest syllabus. In addition to all this, a woman from our church was moved to give Pam and I a wonderful, all-expense paid, weekend at Das Dutch Essenhaus Inn in Middlebury, Indiana which included a marvelous buffet dinner and breakfast!

We have learned you cannot out give God and He truly wants us to break every curse of poverty and walk in the blessing of abundance.

Breaking the Curse and Invoking the Blessing:

- Father, I confess and repent of withholding my full tithe from You.
- I have trusted my stinginess more than I have trusted your generosity.
- I ask You to remove every spirit of mental poverty from me and correct my mindset concerning earning, spending, and giving. (Expel!)
- Please show me where and when You want me to sow seed in good soil and teach me to trust You to multiply all seed sown.
- I declare, according to Luke 6:38, that I can never out give you and with the measure I use it will be measured back to me. Amen.

Since these earlier lessons, Heavenly Father has taught us many more lessons. In 2022 I authored a 225-page book, *Kingdom Abundance: Unlocking Heaven's Mindset on Finances.*

I recommend this book for people who want to move beyond breaking curses over their finances to move into fullness of blessing.

Using these principles which the Lord has taught, we have been free from debt since 2014 and have been able to pay cash for everything, including big ticket items like cars and trucks. Even more exciting, we have been able truly bless our home church and other ministries.

China Inland Mission Founder Hudson Taylor famously said,

God's work, done God's way, will never lack God's resources.

Endnotes:
[1] answersingenesis.org/.../the-splendor-of-thorns by Jud Davis on May 27, 2009; last featured April 15, 2012.
[2] Larry Huch, The 7 Places Jesus Shed His Blood. Whitaker House, 2000, 2004, page 60.

CHAPTER SEVEN
TAKING BACK SUCCESS THROUGH HIS HANDS
From Disappointment to Divine Appointment!

Look at your hands and consider the following questions. Do you have blessed hands or cursed hands? Have your hands prospered and brought blessings to you or others—or have they been used of the enemy to steal, kill, and destroy?

Regardless of how your hands have been used in the past—they can be blessed from here on. The night before writing this, it was my turn to preach at the Branch County Jail. I wanted to preach on taking back success through the blood from Jesus' hands. After a song, Chaplain Carl shared a Scripture, took prayer requests, and prayed before I preached. He told us to turn to Philippians 4 and I saw a note I had put in my "preaching Bible" and forgotten. That note changed the whole mood of my message:

> **When you focus on Jesus' scars, it leads to victory.**
> **When you focus on your own scars, it leads to defeat.**

Many of the dear men participating in that jail service were there because of things they had done with their hands! Whether using or manufacturing drugs, stealing, some form of physical abuse or excessive drinking—their hands had brought curse rather than blessing. If they—if we—obsess over the wrong things we have done with our hands, it will lead to defeat. If we look at the scars on Jesus' hands, however, and apply the blood from His hands, we will enter victory!

When the first Adam was created, he ruled with his hands. Everything he put his hands on prospered. He was able to take dominion and subdue the earth, but when he stretched out his hand and took the forbidden fruit, his blessed hands were cursed. Unfortunately, his curse and iniquity passed down to his own children and the entire human race. The wages of sin soon brought death as Adam's oldest son murdered his younger brother. People began failing for the first time. Projects were started but not finished. Idle hands became the devil's workshop.

Thankfully, Jesus' blood can reverse that curse! Jesus' hands were pierced to break the curse against the work of our hands in order to bring us into fullness.

Human hands can be a marvelous blessing or a horrible curse to us and to others. Do you struggle with disappointment? I like to present that as "Dis – appointment." Most people have thus struggled since sin brought a curse against the work of our hands. God genuinely wants to break the "dis" off His "appointment" for our lives and the work of our hands.

Jesus, the second Adam, redeemed back for us the power to use our hands to bless rather than to hurt, and to prosper through the work of our hands. But we need to apply the blood from His bleeding hands to break every curse against the work of our hands.

Human hands can be marvelous. I love watching my wife's hands as she plays the piano. It is fascinating to watch the hands of people while they are worshipping with hands lifted to the Lord, or on their instruments. The connection between heart, brain, and hands in producing music is awesome as it draws you to the heart of God! Watching the hands of an artist, a carpenter, a mechanic, or a mother with her baby is amazing.

Human hands can also be cruel and horrible. I once sat at a table with a young girl. Every time her father moved his hands to take a bite of food, she flinched. God created hands to minister love, to create and produce wealth, for prayer and praise, and to do the works of Jesus. The devil wants to use them to steal, kill, and destroy. There are over 2,100 Bible verses with the word "hand" or "hands." There is a great contrast between "blessed hands and "cursed hands." Consider the work of your own hands as you look at this comparative list of blessed hands versus cursed hands:

BLESSED HANDS:	CURSED HANDS:
Are comforting	Are traumatizing
Protect others	Murderous
May be guided by angels	Idolatrous
Innocent	Deceptive
May help others	May harm others
Responsible	Irresponsible
Guided by God	Controlled by anger
Spread out to release miracles	Destructive
Prepare acceptable sacrifice	Unacceptable offerings
Sanctified by blood	Unclean
Bless others	Curse others
Release anointing	Entrap people
Set people/things apart for God	The devil's workshop
Bear good testimony	Release fear
Rejoice in the Lord	Wring in despair
Blessed by God for good works	Cursed
Productive for good.	Cause trouble

Their works are blessed by God.	Evil recompense
Please the Lord	Provoke the Lord
Strengthened for victory	Victimized
Diligent	Lazy
Lifted to the Lord	Lifted to self
Holy hands	Unholy
Laying on to release Holy Spirit	Spoil others
Laying to release spiritual gifts.	Take from others.

Are your hands blessed or cursed? Consider the following:

 📖 But his bow remained in strength, And the arms of *his hands were made strong* by the hands of the Mighty God of Jacob (From there is the Shepherd, the Stone of Israel). Genesis 49:24. (My emphasis)

 📖 "For *the Lord your God has blessed you in all the work of your hand*. He knows your trudging through this great wilderness. These forty years the Lord your God *has been* with you; you have lacked nothing." Deuteronomy 2:7. (My emphasis)

 📖 You shall surely give to him, and your heart should not be grieved when you give to him, because for this thing *the Lord your God will bless you in all your works and in all to which you put your hand*. Deuteronomy 15:10 (My emphasis).

 📖 The Lord will open to you His good treasure, the heavens, to give the rain to your land in its season, and *to bless all the work of your hand*. You shall lend to many nations, but you shall not borrow. Deuteronomy 28:12. (My emphasis)

 📖 "The Lord rewarded me according to my righteousness; *According to the cleanness of my hands He has recompensed me.* 2 Samuel 22:21. (My emphasis)

- 📖 *He teaches my hands to make war,* so that my arms can bend a bow of bronze. 2 Samuel 22:35. (My emphasis).

- 📖 But you, be strong and *do not let your hands be weak,* for your work shall be rewarded!" 2 Chronicles 15:7. (My emphasis)

- 📖 And I told them of the hand of my God which had been good upon me, and also of the king's words that he had spoken to me. So they said, "Let us rise up and build." *Then they set their hands to this good work* . . . For they all were trying to make us afraid, saying, *"Their hands will be weakened in the work,* and it will not be done." Now therefore, O God, strengthen my hands. Nehemiah 2:18, 6:9. (My emphasis)

- 📖 And let the beauty of the Lord our God be upon us, *and establish the work of our hands for us; Yes, establish the work of our hands.* Psalm 90:17. (My emphasis)

- 📖 How long will you slumber, O sluggard? When will you rise from your sleep? A little sleep, a little slumber, *a little folding of the hands to sleep*—so shall your poverty come on you like a prowler, and your need like an armed man.
  Proverbs 6:9–11. (My emphasis)

- 📖 And *through the hands of the apostles* many signs and wonders were done among the people. And they were all with one accord in Solomon's Porch. Acts 5:12. (My emphasis)

- 📖 Draw near to God and He will draw near to you. *Cleanse your hands, <u>you sinners; and purify your hearts, you double-minded.</u>* James 4:8. (My emphasis)

Considering these verses, do you believe your hands are blessed, cursed, or somewhere in between? Jesus' bleeding hands make it possible to take back dominion over what we do with our hands, including what and/or who we touch! When God created Adam and Eve, he gave them dominion over everything on the earth. Consider God's original prototype for men and women.

> 📖 Then God said, "Let Us make man in Our image, according to Our likeness; *let them have dominion* over the fish of the sea, over the birds of the air, and over the cattle, over all the earth and over every creeping thing that creeps on the earth." So God created man in His own image; in the image of God He created him; male and female He created them. Then God blessed them, and God said to them, "Be fruitful and multiply; fill the earth and subdue it; *have dominion* over the fish of the sea, over the birds of the air, and over every living thing that moves on the earth."
> Genesis 1:26–28. (My emphasis)

The Church has understood what mankind lost in the fall.

Unfortunately, we have not understood how Jesus redeemed *everything* lost in the fall and wants to restore us so we can bring transformation to the world.

The whole earth is desperately waiting for the true children of God to manifest His rule again.

> 📖 For the earnest expectation of *the creation eagerly waits for the revealing of the sons of God*. For the creation was subjected to futility, not willingly, but because of Him who subjected it in hope; because the creation itself also will be delivered from the bondage of corruption into the glorious liberty of the children of God. For we know that the whole creation groans and labors with birth pangs together until now. Not only that, but we also who have the firstfruits of the Spirit, even we ourselves groan within ourselves, eagerly waiting for the adoption, the redemption of our body.
> Romans 8:19–23. (My emphasis)

The fullness of the sons of God will not be completed until Jesus returns as conquering King, but we certainly are called to live and rule as the children of God.

In the parable about the minas Jesus mentioned the landowner told his tenants to "occupy until I come" (Luke 19:13). This parable shows the Lord does not want us to hand the whole world over to the devil in a handbasket. He wants us, as the children of God, to forcibly advance His Kingdom on this earth (Matthew 11:12).

> From the days of John the Baptist until now the kingdom of heaven suffers violent assault, and violent men seize it by force [as a precious prize]. Matthew 11:12 AMP.

Jesus took back everything Adam lost through the fall, by redeeming it for us through His blood! Psalm 68:18 implies Jesus *received gifts from* men. Ephesians 4:8 says Jesus *gave gifts* to men. Somewhere between Jesus' crucifixion and ascension, Jesus took back the dominion and authority humans forfeited through sin, so He might restore it to His Apostolic Church! I will share more on this in the next chapter.

Adam was cursed and his ground was cursed but Jesus bought the blessing back for us and gives us opportunity to take it back for ourselves through His blood.

The life of the Patriarch Joseph demonstrates how God can and will bless the work of those who will truly serve God through their work.

> And his master saw that the Lord was with him and that *the Lord made all he did to prosper in his hand.* Genesis 39:3.
> (My emphasis)

If God so blessed the work of Joseph's hands after God cursed the ground in Adam's day, and after He covered the earth with water during Noah's day, can He not bless the work of our hands in our day?

Before Jesus' hands were nailed to the cross, He used them to heal the sick, multiply the loaves and fishes, raise the dead to life, comfort the grieving, and bless the children.

On the cross, Jesus' hands were left powerless. He could barely pull Himself up to gasp a breath of air because of the pain of pulling against His pierced hands.

When those spikes were driven into Jesus' hands and His blood spilled from them, He broke the curse against the work of our hands and bought back our dominion and authority, so we can rule in and for the Kingdom.

Jesus' hands bled; therefore, we can lay hands on the sick and they will be healed.

There are times when my hands feel like they are burning with anointing to heal and deliver, and we have a granddaughter whose hands began burning with anointing as she laid her hands on the sick when she was fourteen.

We can lift up our hands and tell demons to flee. (Keep your faith focused on the Lord, not the heat in your hands!)

Jesus' hands bled, we can lay hands on the empty and they will be filled. We can raise holy hands in prayer and see great things happen.

At one time our small city had a house of prostitution. It went under the guise of a health spa and massage center. Chief Ally, our then Police Chief, told the Minister's Association he wasn't able to do anything about it. He knew what was going on there and even said the only Health issue there was the STD's people carried after they visited the spa. But he couldn't find a credible witness of what went on there, though he had plenty of volunteers. So, my prayer partner, some Kingdom-minded pastors, and I prayed around that building the police could not shut down. Within weeks it was closed. We've had similar success with two bars who were known for their perversity.

Because of what Jesus did—we can take back our authority and rule with our hands. Think of the power a 190-pound policeman has to stop an 80,000 pound 18-wheeler. He can do so because of the authority invested in him.

Jesus delegated His authority and power to us! Once I took a giant of a man through deliverance. He probably outweighed me by 150 pounds, and the demon in him stirred him to jump out of his chair so hard it shattered into pieces. He instantly stood in front of me, and I think the demon manifesting through him wanted to kill me, but I raised my hand and quietly but firmly said, "Stop it!" I then pulled up a steel chair and told him to sit down. He complied but ripped his long-sleeved shirt off, began flexing his muscles, and singing "Jesus loves me" in a mocking voice. I cast the demon out of him, and he began weeping repentantly. How could I do that? By using the authority Jesus redeemed back for me through His bleeding hands.

Jesus' hands bled to break the curse against our creativity and productivity. We must intentionally apply His blood to break the curse against the work of our hands, and bless them to do the works Jesus did and even greater things than those (John 14:12).

The precious blood from Jesus' bleeding hands is power to release a blessing over the work of our hands so we too may work miracles, multiply wealth, meet personal needs and bless others with need. It is impossible to please God without faith, however.

We must purposely invoke God's blessing over our hands and work.

Breaking the Curse and Invoking the Blessing:

- In Jesus' Name I apply the drops from Jesus' Bleeding Hands and take back dominion over everything I touch and attempt with my hands.
- I break the power of every curse against the work of my hands, or the ability to use my hands to create wealth and bless others.
- I break every curse against my creativity and productivity.
- I declare my hands are redeemed by the blood of the Lamb from the hand of the enemy!
- I cast out every demon working against my authority to use my hands for God's purposes. (Expel!)
- I invoke Abba Father's blessing over my hands so I can bless my family, my church, and the world.
- I invoke Jesus' blessing over everything I lay my hands to.
- Father, make my hands creative and productive for You and Your Kingdom.
- In Jesus' Name and through the blood from His nail pierced hands. Amen.

Chapter Eight
Taking Back Dominion Through His Feet
From Victimized to Victorious!

Have you ever noticed how some people can speak quietly and people follow their directions, while others yell and scream and no one pays attention? In some homes one parent has obedient children and the other has disobedient children, and they are the same children!

Jesus said, "All authority in heaven and on earth has been given to me, therefore go and make disciples of all nations" (Matthew 28:18–19). Jesus wants us to forcefully advance His Kingdom through the authority He has delegated to us. So why are there some Christians who can't even take authority over a headache? I believe it is a matter of breaking the curse against one's authority and taking back the authority Jesus redeemed for us.

Adam lost his dominion and authority in the garden through sin. He could no longer keep weeds and thistles at bay or even keep his oldest son from murdering his second son. God wants His people to be the head and not the tail, but that level of dominion only comes with the level of authority only made possible through application of the blood of Jesus! Since Jesus bought back for us the authority Adam lost, it is about time we apply these truths and learn to walk in them.

We are called to use His delegated authority to win the lost, equip the saved, and make true disciples, but it doesn't stop there. Rather than let the world mold us into its systems, we are to forcibly advance the Kingdom in every segment of society including families, government, religion, business, education, arts and entertainment and media.

We are commissioned by King Jesus to carry His authority into places where we work and shop and play to impact all those places with Kingdom life and values. Church is good, but Jesus preached the Kingdom! He told us to use the authority granted to us to advance His Kingdom on earth. Early in His ministry Jesus taught it will take forceful men and women to lay hold of the dominion and rule of the Kingdom of Heaven.

> From the days of John the Baptist until now, the kingdom of heaven has been forcefully advancing, and *forceful men lay hold of it.* Matthew 11:12 NIV. (My emphasis)

In the Old Testament, Kings would be deposed by putting feet on their necks (Joshua 10:24). Better than a knockout in boxing, victorious Kings would have their soldiers put their feet on the necks of defeated kings. Bill Hamon had a dream about this and spoke about it in the article to the Elijah list on November 13, 2007. *"IT'S TIME to PUT OUR FEET on the NECK of the ENEMY."* He exposed five enemies whose necks we need to put our feet on. Let me quote from his article.

Five Spirits Being Exposed

We knew the Lord was telling us that we have victory over these five "kings" (demonic spirits) that have been coming against us. Jane Hamon helped research the meaning of each of the king's names to understand the spiritual implications for the Body of Christ today. As you read these brief descriptions of each of them, consider how these spirits may have had access to your life: Adoni-Zedek, king of Jerusalem (this is before the Israelites took possession), represents a spirit of oppression that leads to injustice, fear, poverty, confusion and defeat. This spirit is after your peace and tries to instill worry and fear. The oppression can cause head pain and constriction in the chest.

Hoham, king of Hebron, represents the spirit of religion, which drives people into religious performance to try to perfect themselves through legalism rather than the leading of the Holy Spirit. This can lead to passivity, retreat, moral corruption, exhaustion, weariness and broken relationships. It causes an inability to move forward in the things of God and will always resist spiritual warfare.

Piram, king of Jarmuth, represents a spirit of besiegement that can lead to barrenness, poverty, isolation, and death. It wants to keep you wild, unbridled and too proud to submit to true spiritual authority so that you will be isolated.

Japhia, king of Lachish, represents a spirit of blindness. This spirit will try to get you to shine the light on yourself and demand your rights, so that you take God's glory for yourself and lose the ability to receive revelation from God. It can darken your spiritual understanding, bringing a lack of joy and a feeling of bondage.

Debir, king of Eglon, represents a spirit of accusation. It seeks to get you to attack others' reputations, to bring discredit to leaders, and to stop true prophetic revelation from going forth or to release false prophets. Its goal is to cut off the voice of the Lord, stop the war cry of the saints and remove the presence of God from your midst.

> After Joshua and the Israelites defeated the Amorite armies, Joshua had the five kings removed from the cave. Joshua asked his military captains to put their feet on the necks of the five kings. This is what the Holy Spirit is saying to each of us: "I have given you the victory over these spirits that have come against you and tried to bring you into a place of decrease. It's time to put your feet on the neck of the enemy and enforce your victory!"

I appreciate Bill and Jane Hamon's encouragement for Believer's to exercise authority against the powers of darkness. God promised Joshua could take possession of the land everywhere he walked in authority.

📖 Every place on which the sole of your foot treads shall be yours: Deuteronomy 11:24a.

The word translated "set" in the NIV or "tread" in the KJV is the Hebrew word "darak." It is a word that denotes great authority. It isn't merely taking a walk but putting your foot down. It means forcibly advancing the kingdom. It is the same word that is used in Hebrew armies. When a corporal or Sergeant cries out "darak," soldiers mount their weapons for war.

When we prayer walk our neighborhoods, we are putting this principle to practice. We pray against the things that bring darkness and pray for the things which spread the light of the Kingdom.

If we are going to break curses and invoke blessings, we need to use the blood Jesus shed from His feet to break every curse against our dominion and invoke His Kingdom blessing and authority.

One year while I was studying apostolic church government, I came across what appeared to be a contradiction in Scripture. I mentioned this in the last chapter but want to cover it more thoroughly here. I was studying Ephesians chapter four and followed the cross reference to Psalm 68.

Psalm 68:18 to Ephesians 4:8 both speak of God dwelling on earth with one notable difference.

- This is why it says: "When he ascended on high, he took many captives *and gave gifts to his people."* Ephesians 4:8 NIV.

- When you ascended on high, you took many captives; *you received gifts from people,* even from the rebellious--that you, Lord God, might dwell *there.* Psalm 68:18 NIV.
(My emphasis)

What really caught my attention is the use of the word *"received"* in Psalm 68 and having it replaced with the word *"gave"* in Ephesians 4. Since Holy Spirit inspired those who wrote the Scripture, I asked Him why He used "received" in the Psalm and "gave" in Ephesians. Here is what I sensed Jesus saying.

I paid the total price for the sin of the world on the Cross. I spent eternity in hell over the next three days. While there I took back the authority and dominion Satan usurped through man's rebellion. I said, "give it back!" Then when I ascended, I established apostolic government for My Church and gave back to Kingdom people the gifts of Kingdom authority and dominion I redeemed for them.

Psalm 68 refers to when Jesus died, and I believe, visited hell. Jesus took back the dominion and authority the devil usurped through rebellious people. He took back the dominion Adam and Eve lost. He redeemed the dominion Saul forsook. Jesus so completely bought back the human authority and dominion mankind lost that He could release the Great Commission along with the authority to fulfil it!

When Jesus ascended into heaven, He took those mantles of dominion and authority He redeemed with blood and restored them to Kingdom people through apostolic kingdom authority. Now He says, "All authority has been given unto me, therefore go!" (Matthew 28:18–19) Let me show you the extent in which Jesus wants us to operate in His authority.

> "Most assuredly, I say to you, he who believes in Me, the works that I do he will do also; and greater works than these he will do, because I go to My Father. And whatever you ask in My name, that I will do, that the Father may be glorified in the Son. If you ask anything in My name, I will do it.
> John 14:12–14.

Jesus bought back for us the authority Adam lost! We can apply this concept to winning our children back to the Lord, prayer walking around our schools or community, or whatever. Jesus won back our authority to take dominion. (Prayer-walking is simply walking and praying over things we see or sense as we are walking past homes, schools, neighborhoods, and the like.)

We are not little baby Christians who have accepted little baby Jesus into our little baby hearts. We are men and women of God who have the authority to take back our families, schools, cities, government, and country for the King of Kings!

Most translations of Psalm 8:5 have a glaring mistake based, I believe, on the devil's attempt to keep us from realizing we can walk in restored dominion and authority because of what Jesus did. It seems far too easy to throw up our hands thinking we can't do anything about the mess the world is in, so why try? Let me share Psalm 8:5 from the New King James Version along with its footnote.

📖 For You have made him *a little lower than the angels,* and You have crowned him with glory and honor. Psalm 8:5.
(My emphasis)

The most reliable translations include a footnote stating the word translated "angels" is "Elohim" which most scholars recognize as a name for God. Notice the footnote from the New King James Version. "Psalm 8:5 Hebrew Elohim, God; Septuagint, Syriac, Targum, and Jewish tradition translate as angels."

You may wonder what difference it makes whether Elohim is properly translated "God" rather than "angels." It has to do with dominion and authority. Humans, before the fall and after Christ's ascension are a little lower than **God**. They are **not** lower than angels, especially fallen angels!

When we properly understand how Jesus redeemed our dominion and authority through His blood, we will have greater confidence taking authority over the devil and all his works. Confidence, for Believers, is really faith in God!

Even though Hebrews 2 refers to Psalm 8:5 and also speaks of man being created a little lower than angels, it qualifies it by saying God has put everything under redeemed man's rule and authority.

I find it humorous how the writer couldn't remember the reference, saying "but there is a place somewhere . . ." Look at how he addresses the great authority God has given to people.

📖 But there is a place where someone has testified: "What is man that you are mindful of him, the son of man that you care for him? *You made him a little lower than the angels; (you* crowned him with glory and honor and ***put everything*** *under his feet*." In putting everything under him, God left nothing that is not subject to him. Yet at present we do not see everything subject to him. Hebrews 2:6–8 NIV. (My emphasis)

I kept a Frank and Ernest cartoon posted in my office until it became so tattered and yellow, I tossed it. Frank was lamenting about all the problems of the world and said he was tempted to ask God why He doesn't do something about them. Ernest asked, "Well, why don't you ask?" And Frank said, "because I'm afraid He might ask me the same question."

God *is* asking us why we don't use the dominion and authority Jesus bought back for us. Why don't we manifest as the children of God and make this world a better place?

Why should Christians walk around like wimps? Don't we have dominion? Why should Believers give in to depression, addictions, temptation, bitterness, or defeat? Why should Christians pass by people who obviously need a touch from God? Don't we have dominion over such things?

I was totally amazed by God the first time He told me to heal a person. Even though I knew Jesus told His disciples to go forth and "heal the sick," I never dreamed I was given authority to do anything more than pray for the sick.

I was in the middle of asking God to heal a man and heard Holy Spirit say, "No, you heal him." I argued over this in my spirit for a while but finally relented and said, "be healed in Jesus' Name." I'm not sure who was more surprised, the one healed or the one praying. Jesus meant it when He said we will do even greater things than He did if we only believe. So, do we, do you, have dominion or not?

A similar thing happened with casting out demons. I wasn't sure I even believed in deliverance at the time but kept hearing Holy Spirit tell me to cast a spirit of gambling out a woman whose life was being destroyed by her addiction to gambling. I finally gave in to casting that demon out and the woman was amazingly set free! Do we really have dominion through Jesus' blood? Yes! That is what Jesus meant when He said, "I give you authority" (Matthew 28:18, Luke 10:19).

A neighborhood dog used to bark when I tried to write sermons or minister deliverance. I was never successful shutting it up when studying, but time and again during deliverance I would speak "be quiet in Jesus' Name" and the dog quit barking. I knew it couldn't hear my quiet command, but I exercised God-given dominion and it worked. Why don't we walk with dominion and authority?

Once while visiting an inmate in jail, we were greatly disturbed by a loud and evidently demonized man who was being booked. Even though I was visiting within a somewhat soundproofed room, and the man making the disturbance was at least 70 feet away, the disturbance stopped immediately when I whispered, "stop it in Jesus' name." The demons believe in a Believer's dominion and authority, why don't we?

There have been a few times when God has allowed me to use dominion over weather. The first was just before a church picnic started. We continued our plans even though the forecast was stormy. I watched as the wind picked up, storm clouds gathered, and we heard thunder. I raised my hands and spoke to the weather and commanded the storm to dissipate. It did, and the rain didn't come back until the party was over and the last guest had gone home.

One summer we were scheduled to build a pole barn. By the time the permits were finalized, my oldest son only had one week left when he could build the barn with a little help from me. Unfortunately, it was mid-June, and the weather forecast was for thunderstorms every day that week. Every time it started to thunder or rain, however, I lifted my hands to the clouds and commanded them not to rain. It rained and stormed hard several times that week, but never when we were working!

I'm quick to admit praying this has seldom worked for me when I wanted to go fishing, but every time I've sensed Holy Spirit's leading to make such declaration it has worked.

Think of Jesus' feet. They walked on water! They carried Him everywhere God wanted Him to go. Jesus certainly had power to tread upon the lion and the cobra and to trample the great lion and the dragon (Psalm 91:13). Jesus could walk on water, move through a crowd undetected, stand up to the very men who were trying to kill Him, turn over the tables of the moneychangers and keep on keeping on regardless of what came against Him.

His final steps before the resurrection, however, were to Golgotha where His hands and feet were nailed to the cross. He had been beaten beyond recognition. When His feet were nailed to the cross, they didn't retain enough strength to hold Him up to where He could catch His breath. For a few hours on that cruel cross Jesus came under Adam's curse and lost His dominion and authority. The blood from His precious feet broke that curse against man's dominion and redeemed for us the power to walk in Jesus' delegated dominion and authority. Wow, God!

Now if we will apply the blood of Jesus bleeding feet, we can break the curse against our dominion and authority. If we invoke Jesus' blessing of "As the Father has sent me, so send I you," we will walk in His dominion and authority as we advance His Kingdom on earth (John 20:21).

Breaking the Curse and Invoking the Blessing:

- In Jesus' powerful Name I apply the drops from Jesus' Bleeding Feet to regain the rule wherever I tread!
- I declare my authority and dominion are redeemed by the blood of the Lamb from the hand of the enemy!
- I break every curse against my dominion and authority; first over my own life and sin, and then over where I live, walk, and work.
- In Jesus' name I cast out every demon working against my authority and dominion as a Believer. (Expel!)
- Father, by faith in what Jesus' did when He shed His blood for me, I invoke Your blessing of power, dominion, and authority to advance your Kingdom forcibly where I live and work.
- I take back by faith, everything Jesus restored to His people through His blood.
- I take back authority over sin, disease, demons, and even weather as you lead me.
- I invoke Your blessing to walk in the authority of Christ and take Kingdom dominion.
- In Jesus' Name, amen.

Chapter Nine
Taking Back Wholeness Through His Heart

The first Adam's rebellion brought brokenness and fragmentation to the human race. Imagine how Adam and Eve's hearts were broken when their firstborn murdered their second son. The second Adam, Christ, was anointed to bind up the wounds of the broken-hearted.

We have studied six of the seven places where Jesus shed His blood to break seven core curses and release seven key blessings. There is more healing, power, cleansing, and freedom available from the sacrifice of Jesus' blood than most people even begin to see.

As we look at the seventh place where Jesus shed His blood, consider the following passages: one which records Jesus' death, and two others which predict the precise manner of His death. First, we look at John's words.

> These things happened so that the scripture would be fulfilled: *"Not one of his bones will be broken,"* and, as another scripture says, *"They will look on the one they have pierced."* John 19:36–37 NIV. (My emphasis)

In Exodus 12, God instituted Passover, telling His people to slay a perfect Lamb and take the blood of the Lamb and apply it to the sides and top of their doorframes, in the sign of a cross. The Passover was given to protect the firstborn of God's people and their flocks from being killed by the plague of death of the firstborn. When God saw the blood, He passed over and the plague did not touch them. John 19:36 refers to the unbroken bones of the Passover Lamb.

> 📖 In one house it shall be eaten; you shall not carry any of the flesh outside the house, *nor shall you break one of its bones.* Exodus 12:46. (My emphasis)

John 19:37, which you read earlier, refers to a prophecy in Zechariah.

> 📖 "And I will pour out on the house of David and the inhabitants of Jerusalem a spirit of grace and supplication. *They will look on me, the one they have pierced,* and they will mourn for him as one mourns for an only child and grieve bitterly for him as one grieves for a firstborn son. Zechariah 12:10 NIV. (My emphasis)

A great crowd surrounded Jesus as He breathed His last. They watched as soldiers thrust a spear into Jesus' side and the flow of blood and water gushed out. Very few in that crowd understood the depth of meaning in what happened right then and there.

If you have been involved in worship for more than a few decades, you have probably sung "Rock of Ages." The first verse says, "*Rock of ages, cleft for me; Let me hide myself in Thee; Let the water and the blood, From thy wounded side which flowed, Be of sin the double cure, Save from wrath and make me pure.*"[1]

I wonder how often we sang this hymn without understanding the words. I trust they will mean more to us from now on. The lyrics from another song came to me from my youth. I didn't hear this one in church. It is the Beatles song I remember as "All The Lonely People." The lyrics that played in in my spirit were: "all the lonely people, where do they all come from?" (From Eleonore Rigby.)[2]

As a minister of deep inner healing and deliverance I meet many people who are so broken hearted from past abuse they have trouble relating to their fragmented parts and find it nearly impossible to relate well to God or others. When young children are sexually abused or traumatized physically or emotionally, they cannot handle the trauma. When the trauma is severe, parts of them actually fragment and go into hiding somewhere within their psyche.

This makes it so they can't even relate to all their own inner parts, let alone relate to others or God. Most people have some fragmentation, but some are so broken they have Dissociative Identity Disorder (D.I.D.).

Let me share the introduction from an excellent WebMD article about D.I.D.:

> Dissociative identity disorder (previously known as multiple personality disorder) is thought to be an effect of severe trauma during early childhood, usually extreme, repetitive physical, sexual, or emotional abuse.
>
> **What Is Dissociative Identity Disorder?**
>
> Most of us have experienced mild dissociation, which is like daydreaming or getting lost in the moment while working on a project. However, dissociative identity disorder is a severe form of dissociation, a mental process which produces a lack of connection in a person's thoughts, memories, feelings, actions, or sense of identity. Dissociative identity disorder is thought to stem from trauma experienced by the person with the disorder. The dissociative aspect is thought to be a coping mechanism — the person literally dissociates himself from a situation or

experience that's too violent, traumatic, or painful to assimilate with his conscious self.[3]

So, you might ask, where is this found in the Bible? While there are several verses which speak of broken heartedness, James speaks of such fragmentation, using a compound word he may have invented: "double-minded." James says a double-minded man is unstable in all his ways.

The word translated "double-minded," is only found in James 1:8 and 4:8. The Greek word is "dipsuchos." It comes from two Greek words translated "two" and "soul." A double-minded person is one who has two or more breaks or fragments in their soul. They are hurt so deeply; their soul has fragmented and makes them "unstable in all their ways."

I realize "double-minded" may refer to people who are trying to walk in the world and in the Kingdom at the same time, thinking they can have the best of both worlds. At the same time, I believe it also refers to people who are deeply committed to the Kingdom but are so broken they keep losing their way.

Many people we work with have been terribly broken by pain, abuse, and trauma. They feel rejected and are lonely. Psalm 68:6 mentions God's desire to set the lonely in families. We have a mandate to reach lonely people and set them in our church family where they can find healing for their broken and lonely hearts.

The seventh place Jesus shed His blood provides a cure. His heart was so broken by the pain of rejection and abuse, His blood and water flowed from His broken heart through the place where soldier thrust the spear into His side. The blood from His broken heart is powerful and when applied by faith, will break the curse of brokenness, and release the blessing of wholeness.

Jesus had already given up his spirit when the executioners came by to break the legs of the three men hanging on crosses. Since Jesus had already died, they didn't break his legs, but one did thrust a spear into his side and out flowed blood and water. That burst of blood and water has more significance than most people notice. It was a vital part of Jesus' mission to bind up the wounds of the brokenhearted. His heart was broken to make our hearts whole again!

> But one of the soldiers pierced His side with a spear, and immediately *blood and water* came out. John 19:34.
> (My emphasis).

It is amazing how Scripture was fulfilled when the soldiers pieced Jesus' side. We will look at the significance of the blood and water soon, but first look at how central healing broken hearts is in Jesus' ministry. In His inauguration to public ministry, He quoted from the Scroll of Isaiah 61. His words are recorded by Luke.

> "The Spirit of the Lord is upon Me, Because He has anointed Me to preach the gospel to the poor; *He has sent Me to heal the brokenhearted*, to proclaim liberty to the captives and recovery of sight to the blind, to set at liberty those who are oppressed; to proclaim the acceptable year of the Lord."
> Luke 4:18–19 (My emphasis).

Central to Jesus' mission is healing the brokenhearted. Unfortunately, several English translations of the Bible overlook the Greek word "suntribo" which is translated "broken-hearted" here and in the King James Bible. It means to be "broken to shivers or broken hearted." It can refer to people being broken down personally, or to putting Satan under our feet and breaking him to shivers!

Suntribo is built on two words: "sun" which means "beside or accompany" and "tribos" (treebos) which means a worn path. I testify Jesus is still in the business of healing broken and fragmented hearts, regardless of how long they have been on that worn path!

I spent hours researching why blood and water flowed from Jesus' side when he was pierced with a spear in him to make sure He was dead. I found several scriptural reasons and medical explanations why both blood and water flowed from His heart. Rather than using a lot of deep and detailed explanations, let me summarize what I gleaned by sharing what I already sensed from Holy Spirit. Jesus died of a broken heart!

Jesus, God incarnate in human flesh, had walked with His Father from eternity. He and the Father were one, and nothing could break their oneness until Jesus became sin for us and took our sin upon Himself on the cross. One of Jesus saddest declarations came just before He gave up His spirit. I made reference of this before but will go a little deeper here.

Jesus always called God "Father," always, that is, except when His Father abandoned Him. Jesus truly took our sin upon Himself on the cross and His Heavenly Father turned away from Him because of that sin. Just before Jesus died, he used one of the most generic terms there is for God. Look at it in Matthew's Gospel.

> Now from the sixth hour until the ninth hour there was darkness over all the land. And about the ninth hour Jesus cried out with a loud voice, saying, *"Eli, Eli,* lama sabachthani?" that is, *"My God, My God,* why have You forsaken Me?" And Jesus cried out again with a loud voice, and yielded up His spirit. Matthew 27:45–46, 50.
> (My emphasis)

Jesus, who knew no sin, became sin on our behalf that we might become the righteousness of God through His shed blood.

One of Jesus' disciples had betrayed Him. Another denied Him three times. Family and friends turned from Him. People whom He had ministered to left Him. The final straw that broke Jesus' heart was when The Father did not respond to the His mournful cry from the cross.

That is what broke Jesus' heart. He had been with the Father eternally! That why Jesus could say, "If you have seen the Father, you have seen Me" (John 14:9). On this sad day, however, Jesus cried out with a loud voice, just like others have when they had fatal heart attacks. His heart literally burst when the full weight of our sin completely separated Him from Father God. He was so broken His heart fragmented. At that moment Jesus couldn't call God "Father." Instead, He used the generic term for God, "Eli or Elohim—God."

All four Gospels record the crucifixion of Jesus. To see the whole picture, it is good to study Matthew 26:31–27:56; Mark 14:32–15:47; Luke 22:39–49; and John 18:1–19:47. For our purpose here, I am repeating Matthew 27:45–46, 50 and adding other verses from Matthew and Luke so you can see them together.

- Now from the sixth hour until the ninth hour there was darkness over all the land. And about the ninth hour Jesus cried out with a loud voice, saying, "Eli, Eli, lama sabachthani?" that is, *"My God, My God, why have You forsaken Me?"* Matthew 27: 45–46. (My emphasis)

- And when Jesus had cried out with a loud voice, He said, *"Father, 'into Your hands I commit My spirit.'"* Having said this, He breathed His last. Luke 23:46. (My emphasis)

We should never overlook the other amazing and marvelous things which happened as Jesus died on the cross. Even the Centurion and those with him who had taken part in Jesus' crucifixion, had a change of mind when they saw what happened (Matthew 27:51–54). Look at it for yourself.

> Then, behold, the veil of the temple was torn in two from top to bottom; and the earth quaked, and the rocks were split, and the graves were opened; and many bodies of the saints who had fallen asleep were raised; and coming out of the graves after His resurrection, they went into the holy city and appeared to many. Matthew 27:51–53.

Jesus cried out "My God, My God, why have you forsaken me." The strongest indicator of having a broken or fragmented heart may be the burdensome weight of feeling totally forsaken by others and God, just like Jesus was. How can people return to God after feeling totally forsaken?

Amazingly, Jesus' final words on the cross, gasped after His heart literally burst were "Father, into your hands I commit My Spirit." Even when Jesus couldn't feel God or find Him, by faith He cried out "Father!" Isn't that incredible? Jesus' faith in the midst of such awful pain and betrayal opened the way for the broken-hearted to believe again! Paul wrote "Everyone who calls upon the Name of the Lord shall be saved" (Romans 10:13).

Years ago, Pam and I were talking with Pastor Jack Eitelbuss. Pastor Jack was bemoaning the fact that Christians seldom use the name "Jesus" in their conversations. Even in prayer they usually refer to God using the generic term "god," rather than "Father," or "Jesus." Pam commented, "Maybe it's because they don't know Him well enough to call Him by name."

That is not what happened, however, when Jesus did not use the Father's personal name when addressing Him from the cross. He was separated from the Father as He carried our sin upon the tree. Even when Jesus didn't feel God and couldn't find Him, He still called out in faith, "Father." Shortly after this, the soldiers were commanded to break the legs of the three men hanging on their crosses. When they came to Jesus, He was already dead, so they didn't break His legs. Instead, one of the soldiers pierced His heart with a sword and out poured blood and water.

Some say the blood and water which poured from Jesus' heart give medical evidence His heart was literally ruptured, but we don't need medical evidence to prove Jesus' heart was broken. Jesus experienced continual heartbreak. The crowds took advantage of His blessings but did not follow in faith. He asked His best friends to stay awake with Him during His time of greatest trial and each one fell asleep. His disciples promised to be faithful, but one denied Him, another betrayed Him, and most forsook Him when He needed them most. The crowds cried out for Barabbas to be released and Jesus to crucified. He came to His own, but His own did not receive Him. He saw the pain in His mother's eyes as He hung on a cross.

When you consider how Jesus was betrayed, falsely accused, targeted by the religious leaders, wronged by friends and enemies, scourged, crowned with thorns, forced to carry His own cross, stripped naked, and nailed hands and feet to a cross, you can easily assume His precious heart broke.

At the point of dying from a broken heart, however, Jesus did something amazing which seems to be perquisite to having one's own broken heart healed. He asked the Father to forgive those who wronged Him so traumatically.

📖 But Jesus was saying, *"Father, <u>forgive them;</u> for they do not know what they are doing."* Luke 23:34a NASB.
(My emphasis)

When people come to the point of faith where they will choose to forgive those who have broken their hearts and leave vengeance in the hand of the Lord, they are able to fully receive the work of Jesus, whose own heart was broken, that their hearts may be made whole.

With the blood and water which flowed from His broken heart, Jesus broke the curse of broken heartedness to restore joy and wholeness, even to those whose hearts have been broken and fragmented through horrific abuse and trauma.

Jesus not only broke the curse of brokenness and fragmentation, He also won back our wholeness and joy. For years I thought and taught joy was putting Jesus first, others second, and yourself last but Holy Spirit corrected me. He says true joy is Jesus Overflowing You!

Breaking the Curse and Invoking the Blessing:

- ✝ Jesus, today, by faith, I choose to forgive those who have broken my heart. Vengeance is the Lord's, and I choose to leave judgment in His hands.
- ✝ In Jesus' Name I apply the blood and water from Jesus' bleeding heart to my own inner brokenness and fragmentation.
- ✝ I declare I am redeemed from brokenness and fragmentation by the blood of the Lamb from the hand of the enemy!
- ✝ I break the curse of broken-heartedness and fragmentation in the Mighty Name of Jesus and through His blood.
- ✝ I apply the blood and water from Jesus' Bleeding Heart and take back my wholeness!

- ☥ I break every curse of brokenness and fragmentation and command every demon assigned through that to leave me now in Jesus' Name. (Expel!)
- ☥ Jesus, I now ask you to bind up the wounds of my broken heart.
- ☥ Holy Spirit, I invoke Your blessing of the anointing You gave Jesus to heal the broken-hearted.
- ☥ I invoke Your blessing for my own healing, and so I will be used to release Your healing to others.
- ☥ Abba Father, in Jesus' Name I invoke the true joy of Jesus Overflowing Me in every aspect of my heart and life.
- ☥ I invoke Your blessing of wholeness and joy through the blood and water from Jesus' broken heart. Amen.

Endnotes:

[1] Augustus M. Toplady, 1740–1778. Thomas Hasting, 1784–1872; Hymns of Glorious Praise, Gospel Publishing House 1969. Hymn # 336.

[2] Beatles, "All the Lonely People Lyrics on Demand." "http://www.azlyrics.com/lyrics/beatles/eleanorrigby.html

[3] http://www.webmd.com/mental-health/dissociative-identity-disorder-multiple-personality-disorder

May Hearts Dare To Beat Again

May Hearts Dare to Beat Again

Raped, pillaged, put down, insulted.
Children passed over,
Watching their parent neglect them
While chasing after lovers to
Heal them of their own past neglect.

Somewhere, somehow, the cycle has to stop.
Yet it can never begin to stop,
Until the healing has begun.
To sew up the wounds of the bleeding heart,
And pull together each fragmented part.

Ministers of healing divine yet human,
Must move beneath the surface,
Where the stain of lurking pain,
Makes the heart afraid to beat again.

Oh, where can such love be found,
That makes it worth the risk,
To feel the pain and live again?

Could this be the true Gospel Message?
Love so pure, so intimate, and divine.
That one can open the past
And in the future learn
To trust again, love again,
And risk feeling once more?

Yes, this is the hope, the message and ministry,
Of One anointed to heal the broken heart.
The One sent to set the captive free
And set those oppressed at liberty.

Our world, yes probably those reading this,
Is filled with men and women who continue --
Trying to still the pain of abuse
From childhood and beyond.

Sticks and stones may break my bones,
But bones are easily healed.
Curses, neglect, hurtful words
Along with all forms of abuse.
Leave scars that affect all of life,
Until they are gently opened
By the Great Physician's hand.

Only He can heal deep inner wounds,
Hidden from all . . . .
And tucked away deep within.

Only the blood and water
Which flowed from His own broken heart,
Can flow through my broken heart,
To your broken heart,
Until in Him we are whole again.

~Douglas E. Carr 8/17/2015

Chapter Ten
Praying it All the Way Through

There are dozens of places to learn more about the seven places Jesus shed His blood to break seven core curses. If you put "Seven places Jesus shed His blood" in an Internet search engine, you will find several great articles worth reading.

My Christian life developed with a strong theology of the Word of God. I wanted God to engraft His Word into my heart and save my soul (James 1:21). Unfortunately, it took years before I understood theology pertains not only to the Word of God but also to the God of the Word!

Over the past few years, the God of the Word has quickened His revelation within me concerning how Jesus shed His blood in seven specific places to break seven curses. He has worked in me and through me to invoke God's blessings through Jesus' blood to take back His working to will and to do according to His will. He has shown me how to take back my own health, freedom, prosperity, success, dominion, and wholeness.

This wonderful revelation has become an essential part of nearly every ministry appointment I do. In this chapter I merely want you pray the blood of Jesus over you, and your family, as I have for countless others.

A prayer to apply the wonder of Jesus' blood personally.

- Heavenly Father, I am absolutely amazed You love me so much You gave Your Only Begotten Son so I might not perish but have everlasting life.
- Jesus, You are the Lamb of God who takes away my sin and gives me power to break curses and invoke blessings through the blood You shed.
- I confess I have been selfish, narcissistic, and self-protective. I have built walls around my heart to avoid pain rather than turning to You in my pain.
- Jesus, You were tempted in every way I have been, yet were without sin.
- In the Garden of Gethsemane, You were tempted not to fully surrender to Your Father's will to take our sins upon Yourself on the cross.
- You asked your best friends to stay awake and pray while you were sorely tempted and traumatized. Every one of them fell asleep.
- You prayed, and prayed again, "Father, if You are willing, take this cup from Me." You didn't want to be separated from the Father. You didn't want to become sin on our behalf. You were tempted to not be the Lamb of God who takes away the sin of the world.
- Thank You for overcoming that temptation and praying "yet not My will but Yours be done." Even with an angel attending You, You began to pray more earnestly, and Your sweat was like drops of blood falling to the ground.
- Lord Jesus, I take Your sweat drops of blood and I purposely break the curse of my self-protective, guarded, and self-directed will. I command every spirit of rebellion, every stiff-necked spirit, and every spirit of rejection, fear, and

stubbornness to leave me now! (Expel!) I use Your blood to break off narcissism from my willing, thinking, and doing.

- I invoke Your blessing of God working in me to will and to do of Your good pleasure. Through Your blood I identify with You and say "yet not by will, but Yours be done" in me, by me, and through me.
- Jesus, they falsely accused You, tried You unjustly, and tied You to a whipping post. They took a whip embedded with sharp pieces of metal and bone and whipped you, tearing pieces of flesh from Your body.
- Isaiah prophesied "by Your stripes I am healed." Peter says we were healed through Your stripes. I confess every place where I and my ancestors have given into sickness. I confess where I have looked to physicians and alternative treatment before looking to You.
- Today I take the precious blood from Your stripes and break every curse of sickness, disease, and infirmity. I command every spirit of infirmity and disease to leave me right now in Jesus' Name. (Expel!)
- In Your Precious Name and through Your Blood, I demolish the stronghold of infirmity and command the root spirit of infirmity to loose me now. (Expel!)
- I invoke the blessing of health over me and my family line. I pray none of the diseases of Egypt will ever again visit me or my family.
- Lord Jesus, Isaiah prophesied You were bruised for my iniquities. You bled underneath the surface of Your skin to break the curse of everything lurking deep within me.
- Today, by faith, I apply the blood from Your bruises to break every curse of personal and generational iniquity. I take the blood from Your bruises and break every curse of brokenness, grief, anger, selfishness, sorrow and depression which has held me and my family in bondage. I invoke the blessing of

freedom from iniquity, and the blessing of transparency before You and those closest to me.

✟ Jesus, the soldiers added insult to injury when they placed a robe over You, put a staff in Your hands, and crafted a crown of thorns from the symbol of poverty. You became poor for my sake so I might be rich in You. They took the staff from Your hand and beat Your face over and over again. Your blood poured from the wounds on Your head and face.

✟ I confess where I've sought first financial gain rather Your Kingdom. I confess where I have withheld my tithes and offerings and behaved like I alone am responsible for making it financially.

✟ Today, I apply the blood from Your head where you wore the crown of thorns to break every curse of poverty off from me and my family line.

✟ I command every spirit of mental poverty to leave me now. (Expel!) I invoke Your blessing of prosperity over my life. I ask You to bless me financially and use me to bless Your work and Your people financially. I invoke Your blessing so I may prosper in all things even as my soul prospers.

✟ Jesus, they led You to the cross. They nailed Your hands to the tree. They took Your hands that healed the sick, multiplied the loaves and fishes, comforted the hurting, and did the creative works of God. Soldiers nailed Your precious hands to the cross. You could barely pull Yourself up to take a breath when you were suffocating there. Thank You, Jesus!

✟ Today, by faith, I apply the blood from Your hands and break every curse against my success and the work of my hands. I command every spirit of sabotage and unrelenting destruction to leave me now. (Expel!)

✟ By Your blood, I break every curse of illegitimacy and command spirits working illegitimacy to leave me now. (Expel!)

- Father, through the blood from Jesus' hands I invoke Your blessing over my hands and my work.
- I pray You will bless me and help me twork at whatever I do with all my heart as working for the Lord, and not just men. I ask you to release Your authority for healing, deliverance, and anointing through my hands.
- Jesus, Your feet carried You everywhere Your Father sent You. You did not worry about provision for Your journey. You just went to the places Father would show You.
- You walked on the water. You took dominion over demons, disease, injustice, and poverty. You tread upon the lion and the serpent. You trampled the great lion and the dragon, but they nailed Your feet to the cross.
- I can picture You hanging on the cross with the heaviness of our sin and weight of Your own body suffocating You as You hung there.
- When You tried pushing up by Your feet to catch a breath, the pain was unbearable. Blood poured from the nail wounds.
- I now apply that blood from your feet and cast off every spirit working against my authority, power, and dominion. (Expel)
- Jesus, You did this for me! How wonderful, how marvelous is Your love for me.
- Today, by faith, I apply the blood from Your feet, and break every curse against my dominion, power, and authority.
- Through Your blood I invoke Father's blessing, and authority power and dominion over sin, first in my own life and then in the world around me. (Authority is the right to act in Jesus' Name, power is the ability to act, and dominion is the ability to rule over personal and corporate sin.)
- With Jesus' authority I will be sent as Father sent Jesus. Lord Jesus, I receive Your commission by faith, and I will forcibly advance your Kingdom on earth as it is in heaven.

- Jesus, most precious to me is the blood and water flowing from Your own broken heart.
- I confess my own brokenness and lay my heart condition open before you. By faith I apply the water and blood from Your broken heart and break every curse of brokenness and fragmentation off me and my descendants.
- I ask You to integrate all my fragmentation within me. In Christ I am now a whole person.
- I speak to every demon causing fragmentation and resist you in Jesus' Name and through His blood. Loose me now! (Expel!)
- Father, through the blood and water from Jesus' broken heart, I invoke Your blessing of wholeness and joy over my life. May Jesus overflow through me in everything I think, say, and do.
- I now declare I am crucified with Christ, and I no longer live, but Christ lives through me. The life I live in the body, I live by faith in the Son of God, who loved me and gave Himself for me.

Chapter Eleven: The Devil's Attempt to Obscure the Power of the Blood

For centuries, the devil has tried to steal, kill, and destroy the Church by moving it away from the blood of the Passover Lamb. Many can remember how central the blood of Jesus used to be in worship. I became a Christian in 1972 and memorized songs we often sang in the church I attended as well as in the five churches I've pastored. Consider the lyrics of some of the songs which used to be common across denominational lines. The first one begins with the question only the blood of Jesus can answer.

Nothing but the Blood

What can wash away my sin?
Nothing but the *blood of Jesus*;
What can make me whole again?
Nothing but the *blood of Jesus*. (Chorus)

Chorus:
Oh! precious is the flow
That makes me white as snow;
No other fount I know,
Nothing but the *blood of Jesus*.

For my pardon, this I see,
Nothing but the *blood of Jesus*;
For my cleansing this my plea,
Nothing but the *blood of Jesus*. (Repeat Chorus)

Nothing can for sin atone,

Nothing but the *blood of Jesus;*
Naught of good that I have done,
Nothing but the *blood of Jesus.* (Repeat Chorus)

This is all my hope and peace,
Nothing but the *blood of Jesus;*
This is all my righteousness,
Nothing but the *blood of Jesus.* (Repeat Chorus)

Now by this I'll overcome—
Nothing but the *blood of Jesus,*
Now by this I'll reach my home—
Nothing but the *blood of Jesus.* (Repeat Chorus)

Glory! Glory! This I sing—
Nothing but the *blood of Jesus,*
All my praise for this I bring—
Nothing but the *blood of Jesus.* (Repeat Chorus)[1]
(My emphasis)

The second is a Gospel song that remains close to my heart.

Victory in Jesus

Verse one:
I heard an old, old story,
How a Savior came from glory,
How He gave His life on Calvary
To save a wretch like me;
I heard about His groaning,
Of his precious blood atoning,
Then I repented of my sins;
And won the victory.

Chorus:
O victory in Jesus,

My Savior, forever.
He sought me and bought me
With His redeeming blood;
He loved me ere I knew Him,
And all my love is due Him,
<u>*He plunged me to victory,*</u>
<u>*Beneath the cleansing flood.*</u> [2] (My emphasis)

The third song underscores how the blood of Jesus used to be a major focus within worship.

There's Power in the Blood

Would you be free from your burden of sin?
There's power in the blood, power in the blood
Would you o'er evil the victory win?
There's wonderful power in the blood

Chorus:
There is power, power, wonder-working power
In the blood of the Lamb
There is power, power, wonder-working power
In the precious blood of the Lamb

Would you be free from your passion and Pride?
There's power in the *blood,* power in the *blood.*
Come for a cleansing to Calvary's tide;
There's wonderful power in the *blood.* (Repeat Chorus)

Would you be whiter, much whiter than snow?
There's power in the blood, power in the blood
Sin stains are lost in its life-giving flow
There's wonderful power in the blood. (Repeat Chorus)

Would you do service for Jesus, your King?
There's power in the blood, power in the blood

Would you live daily His praises to sing?
There's wonderful power in the blood. (Repeat Chorus)[3]
(My emphasis)

The devil's attempt to divert attention away from the blood certainly did not begin with seeker sensitive worship. He did his best to see Jesus killed before He was nailed to the cross. Many Jews believed the Messiah would appear at the pinnacle of the Temple, but Satan tempted Jesus to throw himself off that pinnacle which could have resulted in death apart from the cross (Matthew 4:5–7).

Later, the devil stirred the people in the synagogue with such fury over Jesus' works they took Him to the brow of the hill in order to throw him down the cliff, but He escaped the devil's attempt to kill Him apart from the cross (Luke 4:28–30).

You may wonder why the devil was so bent on Jesus dying before He made it to the cross on Passover. It is because Satan hates the blood of Jesus which was shed on Calvary's Cross. He hates that it can save you. He hates that it can heal you, deliver you, and break every curse if only you apply it. He doesn't want you or me to realize how much power is in the blood of Jesus.

Jesus had to die on Passover and His death should be observed on Passover. Jesus had to die on a cross in order to offer us remission from curses for "cursed is everyone who hands on a tree." Paul explains this by quoting from Deuteronomy. Take a look.

> "If a man has committed a sin deserving of death, and he is put to death, and you hang him on a tree, his body shall not remain overnight on the tree, but you shall surely bury him that day, so that you do not defile the land which the Lord

your God is giving you as an inheritance; *for he who is hanged is accursed of God.* Deuteronomy 21:22–23. (My emphasis)

📖 *Christ has redeemed us from the curse of the law, having become a curse for us* (for it is written, "Cursed is everyone who hangs on a tree"), that the blessing of Abraham might come upon the Gentiles in Christ Jesus, that we might receive the promise of the Spirit through faith. Galatians 3:13–14. (My emphasis)

If the devil can't divert our attention from the cross, he will try to limit the focus of Jesus' blood to salvation alone. I have memorized dozens of Scriptures over the years, including a few entire chapters. There is one verse, however, that I memorized so incorrectly that I checked it out in every translation I have.

I asked our people in our church and at a jail service to finish this statement, and nearly everyone "quoted it" incorrectly. Let's see how you do. Finish this verse from Hebrews 9:22 "Without the shedding of blood there is no what?" The way I memorized it was "Without the shedding of blood there is no remission *of sin*." That is incorrect! It limits Jesus' blood to salvation, when it was also shed to break every curse and bring healing.

Some Bibles say, "Without the shedding of blood there is no forgiveness of sins," but five out of six of my favorite translations correctly read "Without the shedding of blood there is no remission." I am convinced that is the best translation. Without the shedding of blood there is no remission PERIOD!

In the scope of the Word of God, the shedding of Jesus' blood includes remission from the curses of a selfish, narcissistic, or self-protective will; sickness and disease; personal and generational iniquitous patterns; poverty; and the curses against: productivity and creativity; dominion and authority. Thankfully, it also includes remission from the curse of fragmentation, dissociation, and brokenness. There is remission of these curses by the blood of Jesus IF and when it is applied. It is no wonder the devil doesn't want us to know the power of the blood of Jesus.

The first and last books of the Bible share how integral the shedding of blood is to Christian life and victory. Revelation 13:8 speaks of Jesus as the Lamb who was slain from the foundation of the world. Jesus dying on the cross at Passover was always God's plan. He knew what Adam and Eve would do. He knew our need long before we had it! He loves people so much He had a plan of remission for people of the Old Testament, New Testament, and now! Even before Jesus went to the cross Father Abraham believed and it was counted to him as righteousness!

God's first use of innocent blood was demonstrated after Adam sinned. I hope we will see Adam and Eve in heaven—not because of what they did, but because of what God did when he made garments of skin to cover their shame and nakedness.

Adam and Eve tried to cover themselves with fig leaves. They are less than 4 x 7 inches and irregular like a maple leaf. They're even smaller than grape leaves! Can you picture them trying to cover their nakedness by sowing fig leaves together? I wonder if that is why Jesus cursed the fig tree even though it wasn't the season for ripe figs (See Mark 11:12–14). Could He have been thinking back to when Adam and Eve tried to cover their sin and shame apart from faith in remission through the shedding of blood?

When Adam sinned, God killed an innocent animal. Blood was shed for remission of guilt and for redemption. God saved Adam and Eve on the credit plan—the down payment was the blood of an animal—the payment in full is Jesus blood!

There is nothing else in all creation that can bring remission. There is nothing people can do to earn remission. Without the shedding of blood there is no remission. In the Garden of Eden God sacrificed an innocent animal to make clothes of skin for Adam and Eve. This pointed to the sacrifice of Jesus, the Lamb of God who takes away the sin of the world.

The Passover is a better picture of how the blood of Jesus works. The book of Exodus begins with the Hebrew people in bondage to Egypt. The Egyptians worshipped all the wrong gods, and the plagues were judgment against demon gods and those who worshipped them. (See Exodus chapters 7–12.)

The ten plagues were God's judgments against idolatrous worship. The first three plagues affected everyone in the land. The land of Goshen, where the Hebrews lived, was spared from the next six plagues. The final plague was the death of the first born of every family and flock—unless God's instruction about Passover blood was believed enough to be followed by faith.

The Passover was instituted to protect people of faith from the plague of the firstborn. Even though the head of the Jewish Year occurs in late autumn, God told Moses that the month of Nissan (March and April in the Julian calendar) would be the first month of the year. Some believe this parallels the time a baby spends in its mother's womb before being born. I wonder if it shows how life really begins once you experience the power of Passover. The blood of the Passover Lamb saves us from the evil one who wills to steal, kill, and destroy. It brings us into abundant life!

At Passover the people were told to take a one-year-old male lamb without defect and slaughter it at twilight. They were to pour some of the blood of the lamb and put it on the sides and tops of the doorframes of the houses where the lambs were to be eaten. The motion of touching the sides and tops of the doorframes symbolizes the cross.

God commanded His people to commemorate this Passover annually for the generations to come. God never wants His people to forget about the power of the blood, but Satan hates the blood.

The early Church focused on the blood of Jesus. On the day of Pentecost, the Holy Spirit fell on 120 people, by the end of the day God added more than 3,000 people to the Church! Within one year it tripled in size. The Church quickly spread from city to city and region to region as Believers preached the death, burial, and resurrection of Jesus Christ.

Think of the power of the early church to heal the sick, cast out demons, win the lost, equip the saved, and bring transformation to wealthy but pagan cities like Antioch and Ephesus. The church was able to change the moral climate of places like Ephesus and Corinth through preaching, teaching, and signs and wonders. Thousands were added daily to the Church because its members understood there's power, power, wonder working power in the blood of the Lamb.

Satan went to war against the blood! The Council of Nicea I was convened in 325 (AD) by Constantine, Emperor of the Roman Empire. Constantine, a worshipper of the sun-god, claimed he 'converted' to Christianity. What he really did was "married" the church to pagan worship of the sun, even changing the date of Easter to coincide with celebration of the Teutonic goddess of Spring, Eastre.

Constantine's reign marked the alliance of state and church. Christians were no longer persecuted by the pagans. Instead, Christians persecuted others (including other Christians) with a zeal and a vengeance that shocked the pagans. More Christians were killed by other Christians in the first century after the Council of Nicea than had been killed by pagans in the century before Nicea.

Just one year after convening the Council of Nicea, Constantine had his own son Crispus put to death. Later he suffocated his wife Fausta in an overheated bath. Then he had his sister's son flogged to death and her husband strangled. It was also during the reign of Constantine that the cross became a sacred symbol in Christianity, just as it had been in pagan religions. (You can study how the cross was used in pagan worship on your own.)

Constantine is responsible for separating Passover message from the resurrection of Jesus. One example of this was in 2024 when most Churches celebrated Easter on March 31. Jesus was crucified on Passover which was April 22 in 2024. How can it be that Jesus' death and burial was being celebrated three weeks after His resurrection? It is because Constantine aligned celebration of the resurrection of Christ with the celebration of the son god and named it Eastre after the sun god.

What happened to Passover?

The Council of Antioch CE 345 said anyone celebrating the blood on Passover would be removed from the church and considered cursed.

The Council of Laodicea CE 365 decreed anyone taking part in Jewish festivals would be cursed, as would anyone who observed the Sabbath.

The Council of AGDE, France CE 506 said ministers could not take part in Jewish festivals.

The Council of Toledo X seventh century said Easter must be celebrated uniformly at the time set by the Nicea decree rather than at the time of the Passover.

The Council of Nicea II forbid anyone who secretly or openly observed the Sabbath to be part of the Church.

The devil has done everything he can do to make Christians anemic apart from the power of the blood of the Passover Lamb.

I have taught on the power of the blood of Jesus to break curses brought upon us by the first Adam and invoke blessings redeemed for us by the 2nd Adam. We must get this message! We need to bring our wills, health, character, finances, work of our hands, dominion, and wholeness into full alignment with what Jesus wills for us—and it will take application of the power of the blood to do it.

Do not consider this done if you are not willing and doing fully according to God's will. Do not consider this done if sickness is reigning in your home. Do not consider this done if you are struggling with the same bad attitudes or stinking thinking as your ancestors. Do not consider this done if you are still struggling financially. Do not consider this done if the work of your hands isn't blessed beyond your imagination. Do not consider this done if you do not have dominion and authority over sin, the devil, and circumstances. Do not consider this done if you are still walking in brokenness.

The blood of Jesus must be applied in order to find remission of sin and to break the power of curses. Think back to the original Passover. Notice how some verses from Exodus 12 point to the Lamb of God who went to the cross.

> 📖 Now the Lord spoke to Moses and Aaron in the land of Egypt, saying, "This month *shall be* your beginning of months; it *shall*

be the first month of the year to you. (Your whole life starts over when you learn to apply the blood!) Speak to all the congregation of Israel, saying: 'On the tenth of this month every man shall take for himself a lamb, according to the house of his father, a lamb for a household.
Exodus 12:1–3 NKJV. (Brackets added)

- Your lamb shall be without blemish, a male of the first year. You may take it from the sheep or from the goats. Now you shall keep it until the fourteenth day of the same month. Then the whole assembly of the congregation of Israel shall kill it at twilight. Exodus 12:5–6 NKJV. *(Jesus, the perfect Lamb of God was crucified on Passover!)*

- And they shall take some of the blood and put it on the two doorposts and on the lintel of the houses where they eat it. Exodus 12:7 NKJV. *(Blood applied in the sign of a cross!)*

- For I will pass through the land of Egypt on that night, and will strike all the firstborn in the land of Egypt, both man and beast; and against all the gods of Egypt I will execute judgment: I am the Lord. Exodus 12:12 NKJV. *(People who do not apply the blood of Jesus come under judgment and curse)*

- Now the blood shall be a sign for you on the houses where you are. And when I see the blood, I will pass over you; and the plague shall not be on you to destroy you when I strike the land of Egypt. Exodus 12:13 NKJV.

God wants to "Pass over" the judgment you and I deserve. He wants us to be free from the power of death and the curse. He wants us to enjoy abundant life. But if those Fathers in Exodus would not have applied the blood by faith, every first born in their home and in their herds and flocks would have died! God doesn't want you or your children to come under judgment and die. Apply the blood! Put your faith in Jesus and His blood. There's power, power, wonder working power in the precious blood of the Lamb.

Prayer:

- ✝ Father, through faith in the precious Name of Jesus Christ, I apply the blood of Jesus Christ to my life, my home, my family and my all.
- ✝ I apply His blood to my mind, will, emotions and memories.
- ✝ I apply His blood to who I am and who I want to be for you.
- ✝ I apply the blood of Jesus to my health, finances, ministry, work, thought life and living this day by faith.
- ✝ I thank you for the blood.
- ✝ I am redeemed by the blood of the Lamb from the hand of the enemy. Amen.

Endnotes:

[1]*Nothing but the Blood.* Words & Music: Robert Lowry, Public Domain.

[2]*Victory in Jesus,* Eugene M. Barlett, 1885–1941. Public Domain.

[3]*There is Power in the Blood,* Lewis E. Jones, 1865–1936. Public Domain.

Chapter Twelve
Tree of Life vs Tree of Knowledge

The Lord has chosen to set up His habitation in you and me through His Holy Spirit. He wants Kingdom people to advance His Kingdom through the power of the blood! We are to feed on the Tree of Life rather than the Tree of Knowledge of good and evil.

God does move into dark places to shine His light. In the first book of the Bible, we see Him entering chaos to bring Divine Order. To this day, God works in and through people who flow from the Tree of Life, rather than from the Tree of Knowledge of good and evil.

Jesus is the way, the truth and life. His Spirit is the stream of living water flowing from the Tree of Life. If we want Him to dwell among us, we must open our secret closets and come out of hiding and pretension and learn to worship God and serve Him in Spirit and reality. (The Greek word for truth implies reality versus pretension more than it does speaking truth rather than lies. Reality for a Believer is based on who God says we are rather than on how we feel or what people have said about us.)

Let's begin with the Bible's first and final mention of the Tree of Life.

> And out of the ground the Lord God made every tree grow that is pleasant to the sight and good for food. The *tree of life*

was also in the midst of the garden, and the tree of the knowledge of good and evil. Genesis 2:9. (My emphasis)

- In the middle of its street, and on either side of the river, was the *tree of life*, which bore twelve fruits, each tree yielding its fruit every month. The leaves of the tree were *for the healing of the nations*. Revelation 22:2. (My emphasis)

God empowered Adam and Eve to take dominion over the earth. They were to be fruitful and be used of God to extend His Kingdom to the uttermost parts of the earth. Their authority, power, and dominion to do so diminished, however, when Eve believed what the devil suggested rather than what the Lord commanded.

God instructed Adam and Eve to enjoy the Tree of Life and avoid the Tree of Knowledge. As you know, they failed and gave into the devil's temptation. They ate fruit from the Tree of Knowledge of good and evil and lost access to the Tree of Life.

I, like many others, slipped out of the Tree of Life and fed on the Tree of the Knowledge of good and evil. You probably have done the same at least once or twice. Knowledge in and of itself is good, but when knowledge comes through soulish and self-centered thinking, it becomes evil because it leaves God out of the equation.

I lived the first 20 years of my Christian life wallowing in the Tree of Knowledge of good and evil. One hard truth about the Tree of Knowledge is you seldom realize when you are feeding from it.

God gave me a dream while I was writing this. He reminded me of what life was like when I lived and ministered from the Tree of Knowledge. I dreamt of when my children were ten and under, and I was their father, their pastor, and the founding principal of their Christian school. The school started small, and my children made up 25% of the school body.

My dream was a playback of when a student left his wallet in a bathroom, and someone helped themselves to a couple of dollars that was in it. I called the school together and tried to scare the culprit into a confession. No one confessed, however, so I went to Hebrews 12 and warned how God disciplines His children as severely as He must so they will repent. I then led them in prayer, asking God to take out His whip and punish the guilty one until they repented.

A teacher's aide took me aside and gently rebuked me for using God to scare the children. I justified myself stating the fear of the Lord is the beginning of wisdom. I now realize the aide had far more grace than I did.

Imagine my woe and shame when the guilty party finally came forward. It was one of my own children! I promptly dealt with the issue, and confession and restitution were made, but I began judging myself as harshly as I did the one who took the money. I figured God wanted to "catch me" for not being a good father and punish me like I wanted to catch the "thief" and punish him.

I called the chairman of our church board and told him I needed to step down as pastor. It was obvious to me I didn't rule my own household well. I didn't want to bring reproach upon the church because of my failure to raise godly children. Thankfully, the chairman helped me realize I had not totally failed as a parent and God wasn't through with me or my children. Since I lived in the Tree of Knowledge, I couldn't comprehend God's grace flowing from the Tree of Life.

I was introduced to the Tree of Life when I took a Wagner Leaders Institute class from Ted Haggard on *Leading Life-Giving*

Churches. That class helped shape my life and ministry. It is much easier to pastor and minister deliverance and deep healing from the Tree of Life than it was from the Tree of Knowledge.

I realize Ted fell. I wept when his fall made the headlines. I was able to pray earnestly for him, his family, and church. I am grateful God answered the prayers of all those who prayed for him from the Tree of Life. Ted has been restored by God almighty.

Since tasting the sweet fruit from the Tree of Life, I don't like feeding from the Tree of Knowledge. But I seemed to have a "monkey anointing," however, jumping from the tree of life to the Tree of Knowledge of good and evil, even though the fruit of the Tree of Life is far more satisfying.

Both God and Satan are at the door. God wills to bring us fully into the Tree of Life. Satan tempts us to live and bear fruit from the Tree of Knowledge of good and evil.

Let's compare the fruit of the Tree of Life and the Tree of Knowledge of good and evil. I have preached on this subject several times and do not remember how much I learned from Ted Haggard's class *Leading Life-Giving Churches* and how much I've learned through attempting to live in the Tree of Life since 2000. For sake of brevity, I will abbreviate Tree of Life as "TOL," and the Tree of Knowledge of good and evil as "TOK."

Knowledge in itself is good; the problem comes when knowledge flows through soulishness rather than the Tree of Life.

Living in the TOL means remaining in Jesus and abiding in Him. It focuses on relationship and communion with the Lord. Life in the TOK centers around religion and rules and focuses more on outward appearance than on issues of the heart.

People living in the TOL desire to draw nearer to God and His manifest presence. As they draw nearer to God together, they experience true communion with God and one another. People in the TOK jockey for position. Like the early disciples, they want the highest honor and position.

People in the TOL pursue love, which comes from a pure heart, a good conscience, and a sincere faith (1 Timothy 1:5). People in the TOK are worried about titles, recognition, and being honored and respected.

People in the TOL humble themselves and look for ways to serve. People in the TOK exalt themselves and want to be served and highly honored as people of prestige like managers, leaders, pastors, apostles, prophets, etc.

People in the TOL bear the fruit of childlike innocence and are fun and unpretentious. Fruit from the TOK might look good and desirable but leaves a nasty taste in your mouth.

The TOL produces vulnerability where people feel safe and willing to confess their sins to one another and pray for each other. People swinging from the TOK build walls of protection and secrecy around their hearts. They are guarded and tend to hold others at arm's distance.

People living in the TOL feel valued and value one another apart from performance. People in the TOK attempt to earn love by performance, hoping others will approve of them. Tree of Life people value people for who they are. TOK people value others for what they do.

Consider how purchase price sets value. If you try to buy or sell a house, there is the asking price, what the seller is willing to sell it for, and what a buyer is willing to pay for it. In the end, the buyer and seller set the value of a house by what the buyer is willing to pay for it, and the seller is willing to sell it for. At auction sales, the true value is determined by what the highest bidder is willing to pay. Consider what God paid for our redemption.

We are so valuable to God; He sacrificed His Son for our redemption. Jesus was willing to endure being flogged and crucified that we might be saved. In the Tree of Life, people recognize how much God values every person.

In the TOL grace stands for favor. Grace demonstrates how God willingly paid the price because we are worth it to Him. In the TOK grace means unmerited favor, treating people as worthless and thinking God rescued us out of pity rather than love. When people truly respond to the grace and favor of the Lord, He gives them the desire and the power to do His will.

The TOL leads to life and fruitfulness. Fruit comes from abiding in Jesus, and even more so, from His abiding in us. The TOK leads to legalism and trying to earn our way into God's favor.

The TOL leads to increased anointing. Preaching is much easier for me since I've been in the TOL, because it flows not only from what God said, but also from what He is saying. The TOK leads to self-effort. I remember reading eight, ten, or more commentaries for every sermon, trying to find something that sounded good. I was able to preach the best of man's wisdom, but usually spent around 20 hours preparing every sermon. In the TOL I'm learning to let God speak through me and sermons come in less than half the time with far greater impact.

The TOL leads to flow. When you walk in the TOL, Holy Spirit's anointing flows through you to meet the needs of people. You may feel power go out, and may even need to rest, but there is great satisfaction ministering in the flow. The TOK leads to frustration, which may explain why so many preachers leave the ministry.

The TOL brings a sense of worth and value. People in the TOL value themselves and others because they realize God does. The TOK brings rejection through comparing ourselves to others.

The TOL increases one's sense of worth. People value themselves and others when they observe from life, rather than judgment. The TOK leads to self-rejection and rejecting others.

The TOL proclaims the year of God's favor because the Spirit of the Living God flows from the TOL. The TOK proclaims God's judgment. People living from the TOL can win the drunkard, the tax collector, and the woman caught in adultery because they value people. People in the TOK simply preach judgment, hoping people may see how worthless they are so they might turn to Jesus.

The TOL believes God wants happy children so badly He sent Jesus to give them abundant life. The TOK makes people miserable because it focuses on judgment and how God turns from sinful people.

The TOL realizes God is out to bless me and others. The TOK believes God is out to get me. The TOK views God as a great policeman in the sky trying to catch people doing something wrong so He can punish them.

My entire perspective of the Lord and myself was transformed when I understood God calling out to Adam and Eve from a TOL perspective. I always thought God called out "Where are you?" so He could find Adam and punish him. I'm sure my upbringing had something to do with this.

When I was a boy, I was forbidden to walk down the railroad tracks from our home to the river. But there was a day when my alcoholic grandfather grabbed me by the wrist and forced me to go to the river with him. I resisted and told him I was not supposed to go to the river unless Dad was with me. My pleas went unheard, and Grandpa "dragged" me to the river. Once there, I was captivated by all there was to look at. Dad soon discovered I was missing and headed straight to the river. When he found me, he grabbed me by the wrist and dragged me home, spanking my behind with his belt nearly every step of the way.

I didn't know my Dad had dreamed of one of us kids lying face down in the river. I assumed he came after me and punished me because he didn't love me and wanted to hurt me. I wrongly viewed God the same way as I did my father when I lived in the TOK.

People often view God the Father in the image of their earthly fathers. I know I did. I thought God wanted to whip me for everything I did wrong, whether it was my fault or not. I thought I had to earn His love, though I never thought I could be good enough to do so. That was not the case with God the Father and the first man and woman He created. So, why did God call out to Adam?

God already knew where and why Adam and Eve were hiding! They lost their heavenly covering of glory through their sin, but God wanted to give them a covering. He did not call out to them so He could find them and spank them. He called out to them so they might confess where they were and own up to what they had done, so He could restore them. God killed an animal, shed its blood, and made a covering for Adm and Eve. He clothed them with cloaks of skin, from a sacrificial animal.

People in the Tree of Life focus on correction, rather than punishment, because they understand God's heart. God wants to correct His children because they are worth it to Him. The TOK views people as worthless and only deserving of punishment.

I've preached at the Branch County Jail once a month since 1987. I began under the late Chaplain Jerry Vercruysse who truly lived from the Tree of Life. He often asked how certain people were doing. When I had to give a poor report, he always said, "Don't give up on them, aren't you glad Jesus never gave up on you?" That is how TOL people view others. They share the heart of the Good Shepherd as represented by the prodigal son's father.

The TOL is life-giving, but the TOK is fixed on right and wrong. Sadly, I confess I reared my children from the Tree of Knowledge rather than the Tree of Life. I worked primarily from the TOK as a pastor as well as the principal of a Christian school. All those precious children, now adults, would have been much better served had I flowed from the TOL.

The Tree of Life develops a culture of innocence in which people can be transparent and unashamed, fully assured of God's love, acceptance, and forgiveness. The Tree of Knowledge develops a culture of shame which tries to earn approval and favor from God and man.

As demonstrated by the Pharisees, the TOK carries the attitude "stay away from me you dirty rotten sinner." Jesus, on the other hand, demonstrated the attitude "come unto me all you who are weary, and I will give you rest." He came to seek the lost and offered Himself as Savior and friend.

Mark illustrates this comparison between the Pharisees and Jesus.

📖 Now it happened, as He was dining in Levi's house, that many tax collectors and sinners also sat together with Jesus and His disciples; for there were many, and they followed Him. And when the scribes and Pharisees saw Him eating with the tax collectors and sinners, they said to His disciples, "How is it that He eats and drinks with tax collectors and sinners?" When Jesus heard it, He said to them, "Those who are well have no need of a physician, but those who are sick. *I did not come to call the righteous, but sinners, to repentance."* Mark 2:15–17. (My emphasis)

A very practical example of this comes from how we treat people caught in questionable behaviors like smoking, for example. People living in the Tree of Life smile and greet a smoker, while people living in the TOK scowl at a smoker.

There was an Elder in one church I pastored who had a lot of great qualities, but living from the Tree of Life was not one of them. We were sharing lunch in a nice restaurant when a person sitting a couple of tables away lit a cigarette. The Elder began coughing in an exaggerated manner while trying to wave the smoke away. He valued his right to eat in a smoke free environment more than he did the person. His contempt for the person spoke much louder than the thunderous prayer he offered before lunch.

"Sinners" are drawn to Tree of Life people but repelled by self-righteous people who feed on the Tree of Knowledge.

People in the TOL move through the Holy Spirit who always manifests love, joy, peace, patience, etc. People in the TOK move through the flesh. They are quick to condemn, unlike Jesus who said to the woman caught in adultery, "Neither do I condemn you, go and sin no more."

The Tree of Life pardons, but the Tree of Knowledge condemns. The TOL produces genuine guilt which leads to confession and right relationship, while the TOK releases shame that leads to try to cover sin and failure.

I personally lived with a stronghold of shame for over twenty years. I judged myself from the Tree of Knowledge of good and evil because of things I did years ago when I lived in the Tree of Knowledge. There were others, including those I sacrificed so much for, who judged me from the TOK and reinforced the impression I was beyond redemption and not worth saving.

I was released from the stronghold of shame after learning true guilt leads to confession, repentance, and restoration. True guilt confesses, "I *did* something bad," which brings God's forgiveness and cleansing. Shame, on the other hand, believes "I *am* bad and worthless," and makes one feel too dirty to approach God.

The TOL brings conviction leading to confession and repentance. The TOK brings condemnation which loses all hope of ever being able to change. The TOL points to a loving God while the TOK points to an angry God.

In the Tree of Life people can receive love, acceptance and forgiveness because they are drawn to the love of God and the love of His people. Tree of Knowledge people try to look good in hopes of earning love, acceptance, and forgiveness.

In the Tree of Life people can run into God's arms, but in the Tree of Knowledge they are victims, too full of shame to even approach God. Such is often true of people who were molested or abused as children. They often view themselves as so dirty and shameful they don't think God even wants to be near them. Deep healing ministry helps them transition to the Tree of Life. Once there, they finally realize Jesus was and is right there with them, with His arms stretched out to welcome and comfort them. The TOL believes "Just as I am without one plea, but that thy blood was shed for me." The TOK offers "Take my works and leave me be."

The Tree of Life presents the Bible as the Word of Life. The TOK uses it as a two-edged sword to cut people down. The TOL helps people come clean with no more secrets. The TOK seems to believe everything is fine and dandy as long as no one discovers your secrets.

In the Tree of Life, you *believe* and become increasingly like Jesus. In the TOK you *do* and try to become like Jesus but end up more like the Pharisees of old. The TOL appeals to those craving true relationship while the TOK appeals to those seeking the "stability" and familiarity of controlling religion.

The Tree of Life oozes life while the TOK oozes death. The TOL pulls others near while the TOK pushes people away. Knowledge in the TOL opens hearts to receive spiritual revelation. Knowledge from the TOK puffs up and cannot receive revelation from Holy Spirit because their spiritual eyes are blind. The TOL produces repentance and hope, but the TOK brings hopelessness and despair.

Let's take a closer look at how Adam and Eve strayed from the fell short of the Tree of Life and ended up in the Tree of the Knowledge of good and evil.

It was Adam's refusal to own up to what he did and what he became (a sinner) who turned away God's correction and blessing and brought God's curse and punishment. Yes, sin does need to be dealt with, and there are consequences to our actions. But when Adam and Eve sinned, God responded to their need rather than their failure. God took an innocent life and blood was shed in order to present Adam and Eve with a covering of sacrifice to replace the ineffective leaves they used to cover their sin, shame and nakedness. The very first sin engaged God's love to make the very first sacrifice of innocent blood to present a pardon for sin.

Disobedience, then and now, brings a curse and separates people from the Tree of Life. We have already discussed the first curse people inherited from Adam and Eve when they disobeyed God and ate from the wrong tree. Eating from the Tree of Knowledge of good and evil drives us away from God even as it did Adam and Eve.

> Then to Adam He said, "Because you have heeded the voice of your wife, and have eaten from the tree of which I commanded you, saying, 'You shall not eat of it': "Cursed is the ground for your sake; In toil you shall eat of it All the days of your life. Genesis 3:17.

Adam was driven from the garden not only because he sinned, but also because he hid, blamed, and denied rather than confessing sin.

> So he drove out the man; and he placed at the east of the garden of Eden Cherubims, and a flaming sword which turned every way, to keep the way of the tree of life. Genesis 3:24.

Our sin pushes God away, but His love draws us near. His only requirement is that we own up and confess sin so we can repent and turn from it. Consider some verses which speak of confession and its link to wholeness.

> Whoever conceals their sins does not prosper, but the one who confesses and renounces them finds mercy. Proverbs 28:13 NIV.

I lived in the Tree of Knowledge for three decades! I did my very best to present a good front so no one would suspect the sin, pain, and self-rejection lurking in my heart. I wanted to look good so God and others might love and accept me. The Bible way, however, is confessing and renouncing sin.

King David was miserable until his friend Nathan loved him enough to confront him concerning his sin (Psalm 51). I believe it was through confrontation and earnest confession and repentance David was able to testify of the Lord's goodness in Psalm 32.

> I acknowledged my sin to You, and my iniquity I have not hidden. I said, "I will confess my transgressions to the Lord," and You forgave the iniquity of my sin. Selah. Psalm 32:5.

Thank God for friends who love enough to confront sin!

In Acts 19 the sons of Sceva tried to minister deliverance from the Tree of Knowledge rather than the Tree of Life and an evil spirit jumped on them, overpowered them and gave them such a beating that they ran out of the house naked and believing. The people witnessing their failure saw how some minister out of the anointing and others from the flesh.

As individuals and churches, we must purposely reject the Tree of Knowledge and return to the Tree of Life. Let me outline a few steps to move from the TOK to the TOL.

The first step is stretching your hand forth and grasping the Tree of life. Adam and Eve were barred from the Tree of Life and its life-giving fruit. I truly wonder if things would have been different had they confessed "Lord, we are hiding because we sinned." I realize innocent blood was shed to make Adam and Eve coats of skin, but perhaps they didn't invoke the blessing of sacrifice, even though the Lord offered it. God made them garments of skin, but they were not clothed in faith. They looked better on the outside but were not clean on the inside.

Jesus is the Tree of Life. It's not enough to just touch him, we must take hold of Him, and remain in Him. Adam and Eve failed to do so, and death entered their world.

Jesus calls us to life by inviting us to abide in Him.

> Abide in Me, and I in you. As the branch cannot bear fruit of itself, unless it abides in the vine, neither can you, unless you abide in Me. "I am the vine, you are the branches. *He who abides in Me, and I in him, bears much fruit*; for without Me you can do nothing. John 15:4–5.

Adam and Eve paid a huge price because they did not remain in the Tree of Life God prepared for them.

> Then the Lord God said, "Behold, the man has become like one of Us, to know good and evil. And now, lest he put out his hand and take also of the tree of life, and eat, and live forever"— therefore the Lord God *sent him out* of the garden of *Eden to till the ground from which he was taken*. So He drove out the man; and He placed cherubim at the east of the garden of Eden, and a flaming sword which turned every way, to guard the way to the tree of life. Genesis 3:22–24. (My emphasis)

It is interesting Adam was driven out of the garden back to *the place from which he was taken*. This makes me think of people who fall away from God's gracious gifts and go back to their old lifestyles apart from Christ.

Paul calls the Galatians foolish for returning to their old lives in Galatians 3:1-4. Hebrews 6:4-5 warns against people falling away.

I believe such passages describe people who begin their salvation in the Tree of Life but slip back into Tree of Knowledge with human knowledge, efforts, and good works.

Since Jesus is the Tree of Life, in Him we take back the ability to live forever. Eternal life is eternal! Jesus died on the cross so we might not perish but have eternal life. But we need to stay connected to the Vine. That is why Jesus tells us to abide in Him.

Abiding in Jesus means remaining in the Tree of Life. When we remain in the Tree of Life, we will bear much fruit. Apart from vital connection with Jesus we can do nothing of eternal value.

The second step is seeking heavenly wisdom. James mentions there are two kinds of wisdom, heavenly which flows from heaven: and unspiritual earthly wisdom which is from the devil. Heavenly wisdom is Tree of Life wisdom. It brings the ability to see things from God's point of view. Proverbs equates such wisdom as a Tree of Life for those who take hold of it.

> Happy is the man who finds wisdom, and the man who gains understanding; For her proceeds are better than the profits of silver, and her gain than fine gold. She is more precious than rubies, and all the things you may desire cannot compare with her. Length of days is in her right hand, in her left hand riches and honor. Her ways are ways of pleasantness, and all her paths are peace. *She is a tree of life to those who take hold of her*, and happy are all who retain her. Proverbs 3:13–18. (My emphasis)

Wisdom chooses to live by faith from the Tree of Life, rather than by flesh from the Tree of Knowledge. Wisdom makes open confession by faith, rather than hiding and/or covering the stinky flesh. Wisdom surrenders and submits by faith, rather than hanging on to personal rights, pride, and living according to the sinful nature. Wisdom crucifies personal rights and actively seeks to follow and obey Jesus and that, in turn, breaks the power of the curse and opens the door to blessing.

Step three is seeking first the Kingdom of God and His righteousness.

Jesus tells us if we truly surrender to the rule and reign of the Kingdom (King's domain), we can enjoy abundant life like Adam and Eve did before they fell by eating from the Tree of Knowledge of good and evil. The fruit of seeking first the Kingdom and His righteousness comes from the Tree of Life (see Matthew 6:33). Look at the following wisdom from Proverbs.

📖 The fruit of the righteous is a tree of life . . . Proverbs 11:30a.

Righteousness means being in right standing with God through confession, repentance and being justified through the blood of Jesus. It also includes being at the right place, at the right time, with the right people, doing the right things, with the right motives as moved by the Spirit of God.

God makes us righteous when we trust Him enough to make honest confession, move on in true repentance, and continue in true obedience through abiding in Jesus.

Step four is cutting off perverse speech and inviting wholesome people to speak into your life.

Jesus said we are acquitted by our words or condemned by them. Proverbs 15:4 says a wholesome tongue is a Tree of Life: but perverseness therein is a breach in the spirit.

I thank God for people who speak life into me, even when they point out areas of failure. We need to speak and receive words from the Tree of Life. This is so important that I included three chapters on the power of words in my book "Beat Me Up Spirits."[1]

Step five is choosing to be an over-comer. We are to be more than conquerors through Christ! Nothing can separate us from the love of God. We can do all things through Christ who strengthens us. Jesus calls us to listen, overcome, and eat from the Tree of Life.

> "He who has an ear, let him hear what the Spirit says to the churches. To him who overcomes I will give to eat from the tree of life, which is in the midst of the Paradise of God." Revelation 2:7.

Perhaps the greatest fear people face concerning the Tree of Life is that others might take advantage of their transparency and vulnerability and use it to judge them rather than help them. Sadly, such is often true of some Christians and churches, but life-giving people are not like this.

Over twenty-three years ago, I realized I had wasted much of my Christian life feeding from the Tree of the Knowledge of Good and Evil. I used to be more concerned about what people thought of me than what God thought. I dressed, talked and acted like people wanted me to dress, talk and act.

I remember how my big sister swooned over the way a new male teacher swaggered when he walked. So, as a teen, I tried to add a swagger to my hips when I walked, so I could be cool too. A good friend finally told me I was walking like I had a corncob where it didn't belong and promised to help me overcome it by kicking me every time, he caught me walking like that.

I went through similar stages as a young preacher. I remember trying to teach, preach, and motivate others like Bill Gothard, John Maxwell, Dr. Donald Howard, Jack Hyles, and other men of

God I looked up to did. God helped me finally understand I needed to become who He created me to be rather than who He made others to be. God is the kind of friend who offers to teach us His perspective of wisdom and foolishness.

Earlier I shared how I judged one of my children for taking money from a school mate's wallet, and how I judged myself as being unsuitable to pastor because I didn't manage my own household well. I not only judged myself from the Tree of Knowledge, but judged other ministers the same way until God gave me greater upstanding of "managing our own households well."

When I studied the Bible through the Tree of Knowledge, I was grieved by the qualifications given for church elders in First Timothy, Chapter Three. They seemed out of reach for me because my children were born in sin, just like me. The verses which grieved me as a pastor and a father were verses 4–5.

> One who rules his own house well, having his children in submission with all reverence (for if a man does not know how to rule his own house, how will he take care of the church of God?) 1 Timothy 3:4–5.

The Lord helped me understand this passage from His point of view twenty years later. A dear pastor came to a Pastor's prayer group who was totally undone. He could barely talk through his tears. At first, I wondered if his wife had left him for the church organist or something like that, but when he gained composure, he asked us to pledge secrecy and admitted his teenage daughter was pregnant. He was convinced their only option was for his daughter to have an abortion so no one would ever know. This pastor feared his congregation and board might fire him if they found out the truth.

I tried to convince him having a child out of wedlock wasn't sin. The sin was having sex out of wedlock, not being pregnant. I offered to meet with his church and help walk the family and church through this circumstance in redemptive ways.

A minister rules his own house well if he deals with such issues from the Tree of Life, rather than the Tree of Knowledge of good and evil. It is so much better to work through issues like this with transparency rather than secrecy. I wanted to help lead his church into the grace which flows from the Tree of Life. I offered to share the first message I preached when I reentered ministry after my own fall. I wanted to preach from John 8 and the woman who was caught in the very act of adultery. They needed to learn mercy is more redemptive than judgment. In John 8, Jesus was the only perfect man in the crowd of accusers. Being perfect, he could have cast the first stone at the woman. Instead, He said "neither do I condemn you, go and sin no more." As Jesus demonstrates so well, true grace doesn't ignore sin but frees people to go and sin no more!

Unfortunately, for my pastor friend and his pregnant daughter, the fruit looked better from the Tree of Knowledge than from the Tree of Life. They kept their secret, took their daughter to a clinic, the baby's life was ended, and the family grieved alone. They hoped no one would ever find out, and perhaps it still remains hidden from people, but God knows.

The fruit looks good on the Tree of Knowledge. It tastes good. But it is rotten. It is tempting to live in that tree, keeping our sins and needs secret. Chasing after titles, positions, and man's approval is as tempting as the fruit from the Tree of Knowledge was for Eve, but it will bring the same rotten fruit. I suggest the following prayer.

Breaking the Curse and Invoking the Blessing:

- I am redeemed from the Tree of the Knowledge of good and evil, into the Tree of Life by the blood of the Lamb.
- Jesus, I confess I have lived in and eaten fruit from Tree of Knowledge of good and evil for far too long.
- Today I confess and renounce the Tree of Knowledge and forgive those who have led me or judged me from that tree.
- You are the Tree of Life. I choose You this day. I choose to abide in You, remain in You, and live for You.
- I ask You to rebuke demons attached to me from the Tree of Knowledge. I resist those demons now, in Jesus' Name. (Expel!)
- Please help me live in the Tree of Life and point out whenever I go back to the Tree of Knowledge and good and evil. Amen.
- I declare I am redeemed by the blood of the Lamb from the hand of the enemy!

Endnotes:

[1] Dr. Douglas Carr, <u>Beat Me Up Spirits</u>, Create Space 2013.

Scriptures referred to but not quoted chapter and verse in this chapter include: John 1:14; 1 Corinthians 5:10; Genesis 1:2; John 14:6, 7:38, 15:1–8; James 4:8–10; Matthew 20:20–21; 1 Timothy 1:5; James 5:16; Romans 12:10; John 3:16–17; Ephesians 2:8–10; Acts 1:8; Luke 4:18; John 8:1-11, 10:10; Genesis 3:9; Luke 15:11–32; Matthew 11:28–30; Galatians 5:22–24; 1 John 1:9; Galatians 6:1–3; James 5:19–20; Deuteronomy 32:47; Proverbs 10:11, 15:4, John 6:63; Acts 5:20; James 3:13–17; Matthew 6:33, 12:37.

About the Author

Dr. Douglas E. Carr was born again in 1972 and entered fulltime Christian ministry in 1973. He worked very hard at ministry and every church he pastored grew numerically, even though he lacked the spiritual depth to lead his people away from the Tree of Knowledge of good and evil into the Tree of Life.

It took personal loss to bring Doug to where he cried out to know God personally. After fourteen years of ministry, he was broken and left "professional" ministry for five years. For Doug, it took personal failure to help him realize just how loving and merciful God really is.

Since 1992 Doug has been on the quest to know and share the love, acceptance, and forgiveness of God Almighty. He has come to know Holy Spirit personally and has great desire to lead people into freedom and victory.

Doug did his first deliverance in the mid-nineties. He soon sensed the call to lead others to freedom and began leading freedom appointments and Free Indeed Seminars.

In 1999, after a forty day fast, Doug was led to Wagner Leadership Institute where he earned his Masters and Doctorate with proficiencies in Deliverance and Intercession. While taking classes there he met Barbara Yoder and soon became part of her Breakthrough Apostolic Ministries Network.

Doug is truly blessed with His wife Pamela, and their five children and twenty-four grandchildren, and a growing number of great-grandchildren.

Resources by Dr. Douglas E. Carr

Devotionals:
Kingdom Thoughts 101
Kingdom Thoughts 201
Light in the Darkness

Deliverance:
Ask the Doctor about Deliverance
Beat Me Up Spirits
Breaking Patterns of Perversity ~ Freedom from Iniquity
Breaking the Octopus Grip of Addiction
Building on a Sure Foundation After Deliverance
Busting Through to Greater Freedom
Divorced! Obtaining Freedom From The Sun & Moon God. Jeanette Strauss & Doug Carr
Free Indeed ~ Deliverance Ministry
Free Indeed from Root Spirits
From Woe is Me to WOW is He!
Holy Spirit as Counselor

Discipleship:
Choosing Kingdom
Defining Moments ~ My Journey Toward the Kingdom
Let's Get Real
Kingdom Abundance

Healing:
Kingdom Perspective: Divine Healing/ Divine Healing.

Names of God – Prayer:
Ancient Keys ~ Special Names

Spiritual Gifts: Of God, Gifts, and Men (3 Vols.):
Ascension Gifts
Motivational Charismata Gifts
Holy Spirit Manifestations

Teaching:
Breakthrough Essentials
Equipping Generations for Kingdom Advancement
Getting to the Dirty Rotten Inner Core
God's Say So versus Man's Know So
Holidays to Shape Your Life and Transform Your Future
Making Abundance a Lifestyle
Parents & Prodigals
Schematics: God's Blueprint vs Satan's Programming
Time to Act – The Enemy Snuck in While We Were Sleeping

Free Indeed Seminars:

- MOD 1 Basic Building Blocks of deliverance
- MOD 2 Deliverance from Curses, Iniquities and the Big Five
- MOD 3 Holy Spirit Mending of Broken Hearts
- MOD 4 Free Indeed From Root Spirits
- MOD 5 From Woe is Me to Wow is He! (CD only)
- MOD 6 Breaking Through to Greater Freedom (Pending)
- MOD 7 Breaking the Octopus Grip of Addiction

Doug Carr Freedom Ministry Contact:
Email: **FreedomMinister@yahoo.com**
Web: **www.DCFreedomMinistry.com**

Messages

Most of Pastor Doug and Pam's messages are available on YouTube. Browse by date at: His House Church Sturgis.

PAY IT FORWARD

I'm absolutely thrilled that you took the time to read this book. I pray it brought you blessings and inspiration.

Now, I have a humble request. Could you please spare a moment to help others discover the transformative power of this book, *7 7 7 ~ 7 Curses, 7 Sprinklings & 7 Blessings* by writing a review?

Your words, straight from the heart, hold immense value. Your contribution can make a significant impact on the lives of those who come across this book.

Thank you for being part of the journey to share these kingdom principles with others.

Go to: www.amazon.com/review/create-review

www.ingramcontent.com/pod-product-compliance
Lightning Source LLC
LaVergne TN
LVHW051833080426
835512LV00018B/2846